quick crochet
for the home

20 Fast Projects to Liven Up Every Room

TAMARA KELLY

 INTERWEAVE.
interweave.com

editor Maya Elson and
Michelle Bredeson

technical editor Karen Manthey

art director Nicola DosSantos

cover designer Frank Rivera

interior designer Karla Baker

illustrator Karen Manthey

photographer Deana Travers

fw
a content + ecommerce company

www.fwcommunity.com

20 19 18 17 16   5 4 3 2 1

Distributed in Canada by Fraser Direct
100 Armstrong Avenue
Georgetown, ON, Canada L7G 5S4
Tel: (905) 877-4411

Distributed in the U.K. and Europe by F&W MEDIA INTERNATIONAL
Pynes Hill Court, Pynes Hill, Rydon Lane, Exeter, EX2 5AZ, United Kingdom
Tel: (+44) 1392 797680, Fax: (+44) 1626 323319

E-mail: enquiries@fwmedia.com
SRN: 16CR09
ISBN-13: 978-1-63250-415-9

contents

introduction

welcome home

HAVE YOU EVER NOTICED when watching your favorite TV show or movie a crocheted blanket slung over an easy chair, lying across the back of a couch, or folded at the end of the main character's bed? That's because crochet is the touch that makes a house a home. It shows that people live and love and cuddle and create in that space. Crocheted pieces add history and thoughtfulness to a room—and not just on screen!

In an era of mass-produced home décor, there's something special about handmade items. Crochet can be the finishing touch that makes a room come together and elevates it to your own personal space! It can show off your sense of fun, your sense of style, and your fantastic crochet skills.

In *Quick Crochet for the Home,* I've gone room by room to design pieces that will work in the modern home and that work up as quickly as possible, so you can enjoy them ASAP. From the front door to the bedroom, each space in the house gets a few special projects. But they aren't limited to just that space! Mix and move these pieces to where they work best for you. I also have some great suggestions for thinking outside the box for each pattern.

Making the crochet patterns in this book is a way to personalize your home. Using your own color palette, you can create a look that's all you, and just for you and your family. Enjoy!

1
LIVING ROOM
in color

Living rooms can be formal or family friendly—and either way, they should reflect your style! Modern color blocking and bold textures are used here to create a contemporary look and pieces that will fit into any twenty-first-century living space. But they don't have to stay there. Throws, pillows, and poufs can come in handy anywhere in the house!

Finished Size

18" (45.5 cm) square.

Yarn

Worsted weight (#4 Medium).

Shown here: Berroco Vintage (50% acrylic, 40% wool, 10% nylon; 217 yd [198 m]/3½ oz [100 g]): #5100 snow day (MC), 3 skeins; #5164 tang (CC), 3 skeins.

Hook

Size J/10 (6 mm).

Adjust hook size if necessary to obtain the correct gauge.

Notions

18" (45.5 cm) square pillow form; stitch markers (optional); yarn needle.

Gauge

With 2 strands of yarn held together as one, 13 sts and 7 rows = 4" (10 cm) in dc.

Notes

+ *Yarn is held doubled throughout pattern.*

+ *Front and back are the same.*

+ *Rows 2-21 are increase rows and rows 22-41 are decrease rows.*

BOLD DIAGONAL
throw pillow

Corner-to-corner stitch patterns are fast and fun to crochet, and this throw pillow uses their unique construction to bold advantage! Follow the color suggestions below to get the look shown, or make it a stash-buster and tie in leftovers from other projects—either way, you'll refresh your space and make it that much cozier.

Front/Back (make 2)

With MC, ch 6.

ROW 1: (RS) Dc in 4th ch from hook, dc in each of next 2 ch; turn—1 block.

ROW 2: Ch 6, dc in 4th ch from hook, dc in each of next 2 ch, (sl st, ch 3, 3 dc) in ch-3 sp of previous row; turn—2 blocks.

ROW 3: Ch 6, dc in 4th ch from hook, dc in each of next 2 ch, [(sl st, ch 3, 3 dc) in next ch-3 sp of previous row] 2 times; turn—3 blocks.

ROW 4: Ch 6, dc in 4th ch from hook, dc in each of next 2 ch, [(sl st, ch 3, 3 dc) in next ch-3 sp of previous row] across; turn—4 blocks.

ROWS 5-14: Rep Row 4, increasing 1 block per row, ending with 14 blocks in Row 14. Fasten off.

ROW 15: With RS facing, join CC with a sl st in last dc of previous row, ch 6, dc in 4th ch from hook, dc in each of next 2 ch, [(sl st, ch 3, 3 dc) in next ch-3 sp of previous row] 14 times; turn—15 blocks.

ROWS 16-21: Rep Row 4, increasing 1 block per row, ending with 21 blocks in Row 21; do not fasten off.

ROW 22: Sl st in each of first 3 dc, *(sl st, ch 3, 3 dc) in next ch-3 sp of previous row; rep from * across to last ch-3 sp; sl st in last ch-3 sp; turn—20 blocks.

ROWS 23-27: Rep Row 22, decreasing 1 block per row, ending with 15 blocks in Row 27. Fasten off.

ROW 28: With WS facing, join MC with a sl st in first ch-3 sp, ch 3, 3 dc in first ch-3 sp, *(sl st, ch 3, 3 dc) in next ch-3 sp of previous row; rep from * across to last ch-3 sp; sl st in last ch-3 space; turn—14 blocks.

ROWS 29-41: Rep Row 22, decreasing 1 block each row, ending with 1 block in Row 41. Fasten off.

Finishing

With WS of Front and Back facing, matching colors, working through both layers, using matching colors, sc evenly around, inserting pillow form before seaming the last side. Weave in ends.

TIP

·······

You can cover old throw pillows by adding or subtracting rows from this pattern to create a custom cushion cover. Use an even bigger pillow for the stuffing to make it extra puffy!

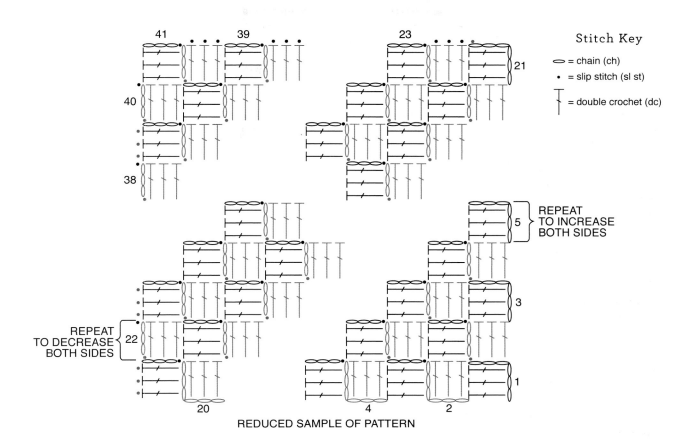

41   39   23

Stitch Key
⬯ = chain (ch)
• = slip stitch (sl st)
⊤ = double crochet (dc)

21

40

38

5   REPEAT
TO INCREASE
BOTH SIDES

REPEAT
TO DECREASE
BOTH SIDES   22

3

1

20   4   2

REDUCED SAMPLE OF PATTERN

Bold Diagonal Throw Pillow

PERFECT
pouf

Finished Size

21" (53.5 cm) in diameter × 16" (40.5 cm) high.

Yarn

Chunky weight (#5 Bulky).

Shown here: Berroco Vintage Chunky (50% acrylic, 40% wool, 10% nylon; 130 yd [119 m]/3½ oz [100 g]): #6183 lilacs (MC), 3 hanks; #61105 petunia (CC1), 4 hanks; #6190 aubergine (CC2), 5 hanks.

Hook

Size J/10 (6 mm).

Adjust hook size if necessary to obtain the correct gauge.

Notions

Inflatable pouf (21" [53.5 cm] in diameter x 16" [40.5 cm] tall); yarn needle.

Gauge

First 4 rnds = 4" (10 cm) in diameter.

Notes

+ *The ch 2 at the beginning of each rnd does not count as a stitch, and is not crocheted into.*

+ *For the stitches in Special Stitches, remember that the post stitch portion will be worked in a previous post stitch, and the dc portion will be worked in a dc stitch.*

The pouf has become a home decorator's staple, and they're practical, too! From footstool to extra seating, a pouf is a great way to add functional color to a room. The Perfect Pouf is a crochet cover slipped over an inflatable pouf, making this project both affordable and easy to move to where you need it. This cover is removable and washable, and ready for whatever your family dishes out.

special stitches

FPdc/dc2tog

Yo and insert hook from front to back to front again around the post of next st, yo and draw up a loop, yo and draw through 2 loops on hook (2 loops remain on hook), yo and insert hook in next st, yo and draw up a loop, yo and draw through first 2 loops on hook (3 loops remain on hook), yo and draw through all 3 loops on hook—1-st dec made.

Dc/FPdc2tog

Yo and insert hook in next st, yo and draw up a loop, yo and draw through first 2 loops on hook (2 loops remain on hook), yo and insert hook from front to back to front again around the post of next st, yo and draw up a loop, yo and draw through 2 loops on hook (3 loops remain on hook), yo and draw through all 3 loops on hook—1-st dec made.

Pouf

With MC, make an adjustable ring (see Glossary).

RND 1: (RS) Ch 2 (does not count as a st here and throughout), work 12 dc in ring; join with a sl st in first dc—12 dc.

RND 2: Ch 2, (FPdc [see Glossary], dc) in each st around, join with a sl st in first dc—24 sts.

RND 3: Ch 2, *FPdc in post st, 2 dc in dc st; rep from * around, join with a sl st in first st—36 sts.

RND 4: Ch 2, *FPdc in FPdc in post st, 2 dc in next st, dc in next st; rep from * around, join with a sl st in first st—48 sts.

RND 5: Ch 2, *FPdc in post st, dc in next st, 2 dc in next st, dc in next st; rep from * around, join with a sl st in first st—60 sts.

RND 6: Ch 2, *FPdc in post st, dc in each of next 3 sts, 2 dc in next st; rep from * around, join with a sl st in first st—72 sts.

RND 7: Ch 2, *FPdc in post st, dc in each of next 2 sts, 2 dc in next st, dc in each of next 2 sts; rep from * around, join with a sl st in first st—84 sts.

RND 8: Ch 2, *FPdc in post st, 2 dc in next st, dc in each of next 5 sts; rep from * around, join with a sl st in first st—96 sts.

RND 9: Ch 2, *FPdc in post st, dc in each of next 3 sts, 2 dc in next st, dc in each of next 3 sts; rep from * around, join with a sl st in first st—108 sts.

RND 10: Ch 2, *FPdc in post st, dc in each of next 7 sts, 2 dc in next st; rep from * around, join with a sl st in first st—120 sts.

RND 11: Ch 2, *FPdc in post st, dc in each of next 4 sts, 2 dc in next st, dc in each of next 4 sts; rep from * around, join with a sl st in first st—132 sts.

RND 12: Ch 2, *FPdc in post st, 2 dc in next st, dc in each of next 9 sts; rep from * around, join with a sl st in first st—144 sts.

RND 13: Ch 2, *FPdc in post st, dc in each of next 5 sts, 2 dc in next st, dc in each of next 5 sts; rep from * around, join with a sl st in first st—156 sts.

TIP
....

Pull this pouf into the dining room when you have extra guests, or make one in your teen's favorite colors so friends have a place to sit in her bedroom.

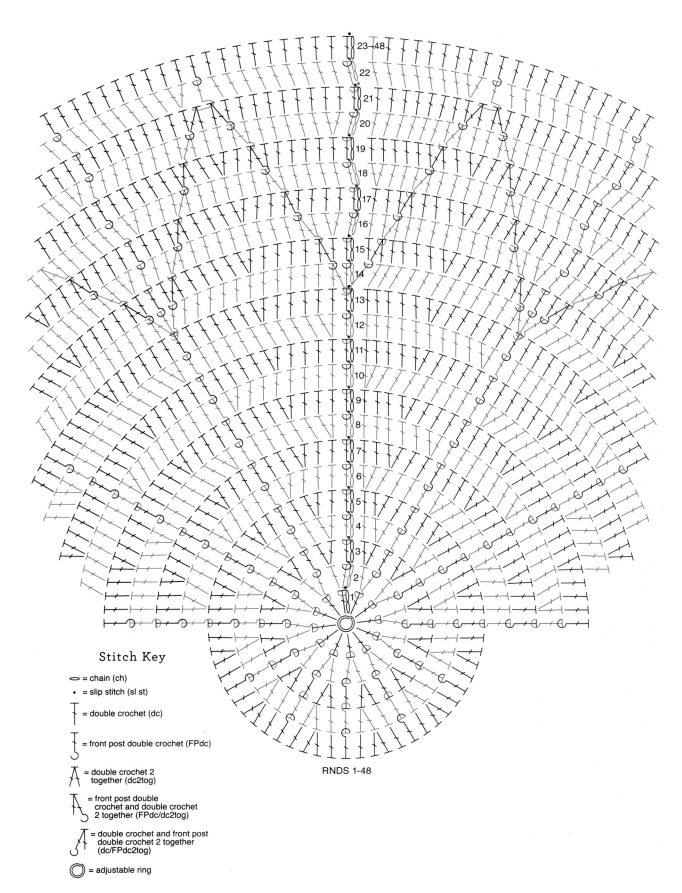

RNDS 1-48

Stitch Key

$\bigcirc$ = chain (ch)

• = slip stitch (sl st)

$\dagger$ = double crochet (dc)

$\dagger$ = front post double crochet (FPdc)

$\mathbb{A}$ = double crochet 2 together (dc2tog)

$\mathbb{A}$ = front post double crochet and double crochet 2 together (FPdc/dc2tog)

$\mathbb{A}$ = double crochet and front post double crochet 2 together (dc/FPdc2tog)

$\bigcirc$ = adjustable ring

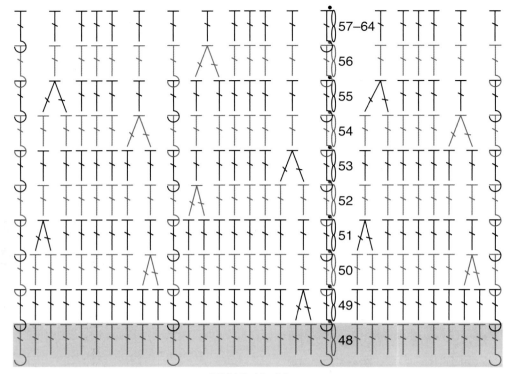

RNDS 49–64

Stitch Key

⌒ = chain (ch)

• = slip stitch (sl st)

┼ = double crochet (dc)

⌡ = front post double crochet (FPdc)

⋏ = double crochet two
   together (dc2tog)

⋏ = front post double
   crochet and double crochet two
   together (FPdc/dc2tog)

⋏ = double crochet and front post
   double crochet two
   together (dc/FPdc2tog)

◎ = adjustable ring

RND 14: Ch 2, dc in post st, *FPdc/dc-2tog (see Special Stitches) over next 2 sts, dc in each of next 11 sts**; rep from * around, ending last rep at **, FPdc in first post st of last rnd, join with a sl st in first dc—168 sts.

RND 15: Ch 2, FPdc in first st, *dc in next post st, FPdc/dc2tog over same st and next st, dc in each of next 4 sts, 2 dc in next st, dc in each of next 4 sts, dc/FPdc2tog (see Special Stitches) over next 2 sts, dc in same post st**, FPdc in next post st; rep from * around, ending last rep at **, join with a sl st in first st—180 sts.

RND 16: Ch 2, *FPdc in post st, 2 dc in next st, dc in next post st, FPdc/dc2tog over same st and next st, dc in each of next 8 sts, dc/FPdc2tog in next 2 sts, dc in same post st, dc in next st; rep from * around, join with a sl st in first st—192 sts.

RND 17: Ch 2, *FPdc in post st, dc in each of next 4 sts, FPdc/dc2tog over same st and next st, dc in each of next 2 sts, 2 dc in next st, dc in each of next 3 sts, dc/FPdc2tog over next 2 sts, dc in post st, dc in each of next 2 sts; rep from * around, join with a sl st in first st—204 sts.

RND 18: Ch 2, *FPdc in post, dc in each of next 5 sts, FPdc/dc2tog over same st and next st, dc in each of next 5 sts, dc/FPdc2tog over next 2 sts, dc in same post st, dc in each of next 2 sts, 2 dc in next st; rep from * around, join with a sl st in first st—216 sts.

RND 19: Ch 2, *FPdc in post st, dc in each of next 6 sts, FPdc/dc2tog over same st and next st, dc in next st, 2 dc in next st, dc in next st, dc/FPdc2tog in next 2 sts, dc in same post st, dc in each of next 5 sts; rep from * around, join with a sl st in first st—228 sts.

RND 20: Ch 2, *FPdc in post st, 2 dc in next st, dc in each of next 6 sts, FPdc/dc2tog over same st and next st, dc in each of next 2 sts, dc/FPdc2tog over next 2 sts, dc in same post st, dc in each of next 6 sts; rep from * around, join with a sl st in first st—240 sts.

RND 21: Ch 2, *FPdc in post st, dc in each of next 8 sts, dc in post st, FPdc/dc2tog over same st and next st, dc/FPdc2tog over next 2 sts, dc in same post st, dc in each of next 7 sts; rep from * around, join with a sl st in first st—240 sts. Fasten off MC, join CC1 in first st.

TIP

....

Inflate the pouf about 90 percent before putting the cover on it, then inflate it fully, tie the cover closed, and tuck in the strings.

RND 22: With B, ch 2, *FPdc in post st, dc in each of next 9 sts, FPdc over next 2 post sts, 2 dc in next st, dc in each of next 7 sts; rep from * around, join with a sl st in first st—240 sts.

RNDS 23-38: Ch 2, *FPdc in post st, dc in each of next 9 sts; rep from * around, join with a sl st in first st—240 sts. Fasten off CC1.

RND 39: With RS facing, join CC2 with sl st in first st of Rnd 38, ch 2, *FPdc in post st, dc in each of next 9 sts; rep from * around, join with a sl st in first st—240 sts.

RNDS 40-48: Ch 2, *FPdc in post st, dc in each of next 9 sts; rep from * around, join with a sl st in first st—240 sts.

RND 49: Ch 2, *FPdc in post st, dc2tog (see Glossary) over next 2 sts, dc in each of next 7 sts, FPdc in post st, dc in each of next 9 sts; rep from * around, join with a sl st in first st—228 sts.

RND 50: Ch 2, *FPdc in post st, dc in each of next 8 sts, FPdc in next post st, dc2tog over next 2 sts, dc in each of next 7 sts; rep from * around, join with a sl st in first st—216 sts.

RND 51: Ch 2, *FPdc in post st, dc in each of next 8 sts, FPdc in next post st, dc in each of next 6 sts, dc2tog over next 2 sts; rep from * around, join with a sl st in first st—204 sts.

RND 52: Ch 2, *FPdc in post st, dc in each of next 6 sts, dc2tog over next 2 sts, FPdc in next post st, dc in each of next 7 sts; rep from * around, join with a sl st in first st—192 sts.

RND 53: Ch 2, *FPdc in post st, dc2tog over next 2 sts, dc in each of next 5 sts, FPdc in next post st, dc in each of next 7 sts; rep from * around, join with a sl st in first st—180 sts.

RND 54: Ch 2, *FPdc in post st, dc in each of next 6 sts, FPdc in next post st, dc2tog over next 2 sts, dc in each of next 5 sts; rep from * around, join with a sl st in first st—168 sts.

RND 55: Ch 2, *FPdc in post st, dc in each of next 6 sts, FPdc in next post st, dc in each of next 4 sts, dc2tog over next 2 sts; rep from * around, join with a sl st in first st—156 sts.

RND 56: Ch 2, *FPdc in post st, dc in each of next 4 sts, dc2tog over next 2 sts, FPdc in next post st, dc in each of next 5 sts; rep from * around, join with a sl st in first st—144 sts.

RNDS 57-64: Ch 2, dc in each st around, join with a sl st in first dc—144 sts. Fasten off C.

Finishing

RIBBON

With remaining yarn, crochet a 70" (178 cm) chain. Thread this ribbon between the stitches of Rnd 64, and use it to tie the bottom of the cover closed after inserting pouf. Weave in ends.

FAUX CABLED
blanket

Finished Size

56" (142 cm) wide × 70" (178 cm) long.

Yarn

Bulky weight (#6 Super Bulky).

Shown here: Lion Brand Wool Ease Thick & Quick (80% acrylic, 20% wool; 106 yd [97 m]/6 oz [170 g]): #099 fisherman, 16 skeins.

Hook

Size P/Q (15 mm).

Adjust hook size if necessary to obtain the correct gauge.

Notions

Yarn needle.

Gauge

8 sts in cable pattern = 4" (10 cm); 4 rows in cable pattern = 4½" (11.5 cm).

Notes

+ *The ch 3 at the beginning of a row counts as dc.*

Super-chunky blankets in neutral colors ooze luxury and comfort and are the ultimate in cold-weather coziness! This throw is a crochet take on that modern look, with a faux cable stitch that makes it as quick as can be!

Blanket

Ch 85.

ROW 1: Sc in 2nd ch from hook, sc in each ch across; turn—84 sts.

ROW 2: Ch 1, sc in each of first 2 sts, *ch 2, sk next 2 sts, sc in next st; rep from * across until 1 st remains, sc in last st; turn—84 sts.

ROW 3 (INC ROW): Ch 3 (counts as dc here and throughout), dc in next st, 3 dc in next ch-2 sp, working in front of 3 dc just made, FPtr (see Glossary) in 2nd st of previous row, *sk next sc, 3 dc in next ch-2 sp, working in front of 3 dc just made, FPtr in last skipped sc; rep from * across until 2 sts remain, dc in each of last 2 sts; turn—111 sts.

ROW 4 (DEC ROW): Ch 1, sc in each of first 2 sts, *ch 2, sk next 4 sts, sc in space before next st; rep from * across until 6 sts remain, ch 2, sk 4 sts, sc in each of last 2 sts; turn—84 sts.

ROW 5 (INC ROW): Ch 3, dc in next st, *sk next ch-2 space, FPtr in next sc, working behind FPtr just made, 3 dc in skipped ch-2 sp; rep from * across until 1 st remains, dc in same st last FPtr was worked around, dc in last st; turn—111 sts.

ROW 6 (DEC ROW): Ch 1, sc in each of first 2 sts, *ch 2, sk next 4 sts, sc in space before next st; rep from * across until 6 sts remain, ch 2, sk next 4 sts, sc in each of last 2 sts; turn—84 sts.

ROWS 7–62: Rep Rows 3–6 (14 times).

ROW 63: Ch 1, sc in each of first 2 sts, * 2 sc in next ch-2 sp, sc in next sc; rep from * across, sc in last st; turn—84 sts.

Finishing

EDGING

RND 1: Ch 1, sc evenly around blanket; join with a sl st in first sc; turn.

RND 2: Ch 1, sc evenly around blanket; join with a sl st in first sc. Fasten off. Weave in ends.

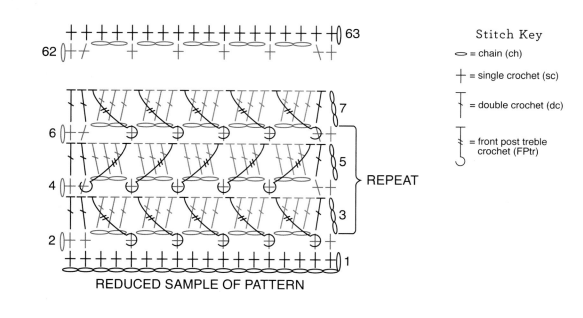

REDUCED SAMPLE OF PATTERN

Stitch Key

⌒ = chain (ch)

+ = single crochet (sc)

= double crochet (dc)

= front post treble crochet (FPtr)

Finished Size

4½" (11.5 cm) wide × 8" (20.5 cm) tall including handle, laid flat.

Yarn

Worsted weight (#4 Medium).

Shown here: Plymouth Yarn Galway Worsted (100% wool; 210 yd [192 m]/3½ oz [100 g]): #1 natural (MC) and #722 sand heather (CC), 1 skein each.

Hook

Size H/8 (5 mm).

Adjust hook size if necessary to obtain the correct gauge.

Notions

Stitch markers; yarn needle.

Gauge

18 sts and 22 rows = 4" (10 cm) in sc.

Notes

+ *Ch 1 at the beginning of a row does not count toward final stitch count.*

DON'T FORGET
door hanger

Busy mornings are hectic enough, and searching for lost keys and cell phones is the last thing you need. Keep your essentials handy with this simple door hanger with pockets for those must-haves. Add one to your front door or hang it on a hook next to an outlet for a clutter-free charging station!

Piece #1

With MC, ch 20.

ROW 1: (RS) Sc in 2nd ch from hook, sc in each st across; turn—19 sc.

ROWS 2-20: Ch 1, sc in each sc across; turn—19 sc. Fasten off.

Piece #2

With CC, ch 20.

ROW 1: (RS) Sc in 2nd ch from hook, sc in each st across; turn—19 sc.

ROWS 2-26: Ch 1, sc in each sc across; turn—19 sc. Fasten off.

Piece #3

With MC, ch 20.

ROW 1: (RS) Sc in 2nd ch from hook, sc in each st across; turn—19 sc.

ROWS 2-32: Ch 1, sc in each sc across; turn—19 sc. Fasten off MC, join CC.

ROWS 33-34: With CC, ch 1, sc in each sc across; turn—19 sts.

ROWS 35-37 (DEC ROWS): Ch 1, sc2tog (see Glossary) over first 2 sts, sc in each st across to last 2 sts, sc2tog over last 2 sts; turn—13 sts at end of last row. Do not fasten off.

Finishing

ASSEMBLY

With RS facing up, lay piece #2 on top of piece #3, and piece #1 on top of piece #2, lining up the bottom edges. Use st markers or clips to hold pieces together securely.

HANDLE AND EDGING

RND 1: With CC, ch 13, sk 13 sts in Row 37 of piece #3, sc in side of Row 37 (handle made), sc evenly along side of pouch, working through all layers as you work down the side, work 3 sc in corner st, sc evenly across bottom edge, work 3 sc in corner st, sc evenly up other side, sc in each ch across handle.

RND 2: Sl st in each st around, working (sl st, ch 1, sl st) in each corner. Fasten off. Weave in ends.

HANDLE

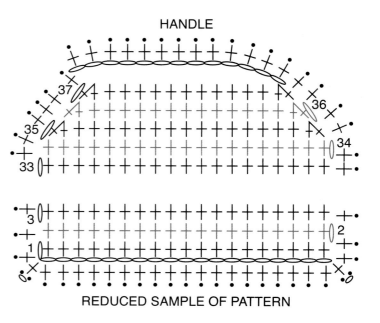

REDUCED SAMPLE OF PATTERN

Stitch Key

⌒ = chain (ch)

• = slip stitch (sl st)

+ = single crochet (sc)

⋔ = single crochet 2 together (sc2tog)

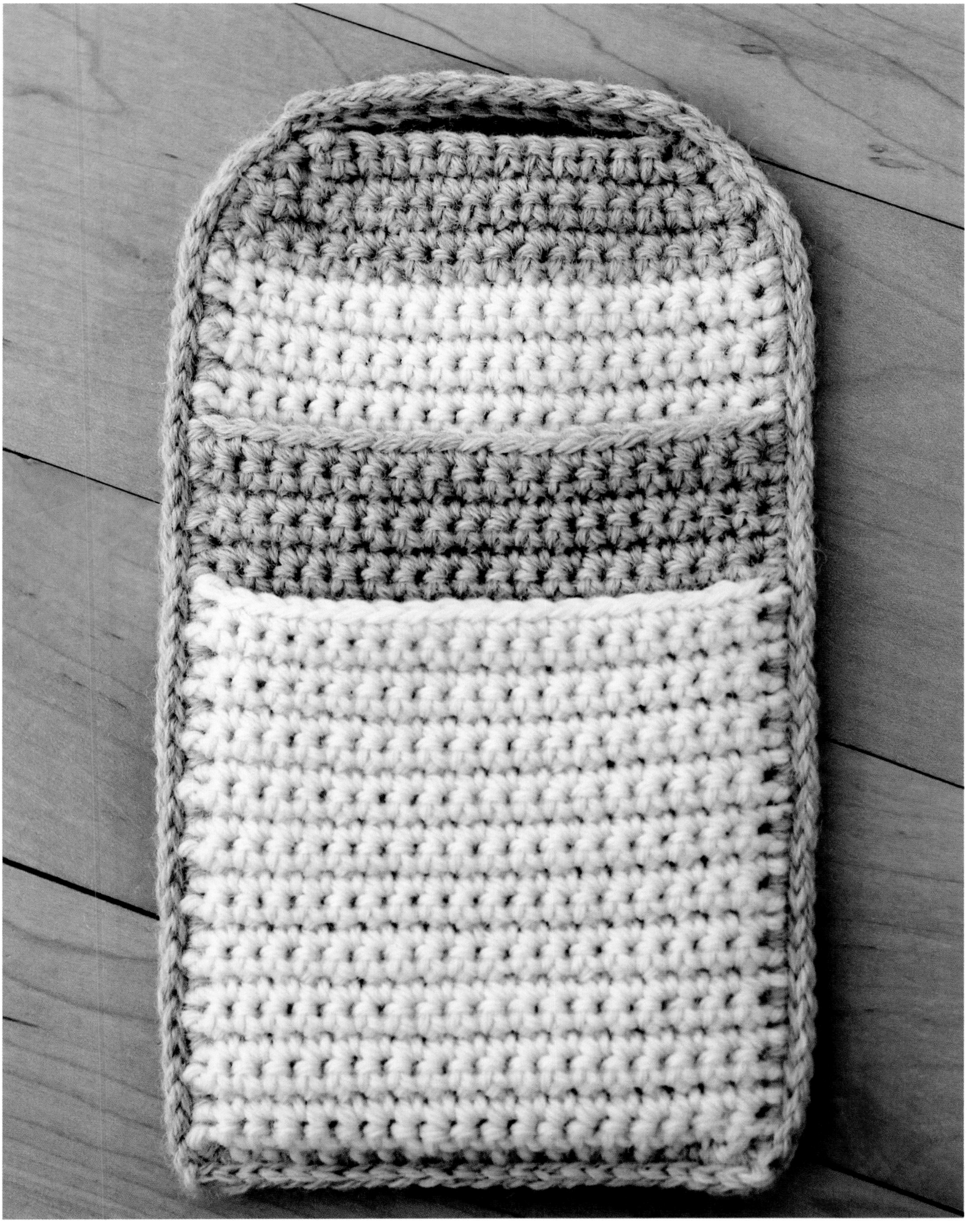

LUXE
LIVING
coasters

Finished Size

Each coaster measures 4½"
(11.5 cm) square.

Yarn

Aran weight (#4 Medium).

Shown here: Willow Yarns Field
(53% cotton, 47% linen; 176 yd
(161 m)/3½ oz [100 g]): #14 iris
(MC), #6 cattails (CC1), and #3
sand (CC2), 1 skein each.

Hook

Size G/6 (4 mm).

*Adjust hook size if necessary to
obtain the correct gauge.*

Gauge

18 sts = 4" (10 cm); 6 rows in
pattern = 2 ½" (6.5 cm).

Notes

+ *Carry the colors along the
sides to minimize the number
of ends to weave in.*

+ *The ch 3 at the beginning of a
row counts as dc.*

Coasters are a great quick project for the home—
to protect your furniture, add some color, or
even to give as a gift! And only a few yards of
yarn are used for each coaster, so you can make
a set with leftover yarn to match any other crochet project in your home.

Coaster

With MC, ch 21.

ROW 1: Dc in 4th ch from hook (3 skipped ch count as first dc), dc in next ch, *ch 1, sk next ch, dc in each of next 5 ch; rep from * across, ending with dc in each of last 3 ch; turn—19 sts. Drop MC to be picked up later, join CC1.

ROW 2: With CC1, ch 3 (counts as dc here and throughout), dc in each of next 2 sts, *working over ch-1 sp, dc in next skipped st 2 rows below, dc in each of next 2 sts, ch 1, sk next st, dc in each of next 2 sts; rep from * across until 1 st remains, dc in the top of ch-3; turn. Drop CC1 to be picked up later, join CC2.

ROW 3: With CC2, ch 3, dc in each of next 2 sts, *ch 1, sk next st, dc in each of next 2 sts, working over ch-1 sp, dc in next skipped st 2 rows below, dc in each of next 2 sts; rep from * across until 1 st remains, dc in the top of ch-3; turn.

ROWS 4-9: Rep Rows 2-3 (3 times), working in the following color sequence: *1 row each of MC, CC1, and CC2; rep from * 1 time. Fasten off CC1 and CC2.

ROW 10: With MC, ch 1, hdc in first 3 sts, *working over ch-1 sp, hdc in skipped st 2 rows below, hdc in each of next 5 sts; rep from * across until 4 sts remain, hdc in skipped st 2 rows below, hdc in each of last 3 sts; turn. Do not fasten off MC.

Finishing

EDGING

With MC, ch 1, sc evenly around, working 3 sc in each corner, join with a sl st in first sc. Weave in ends.

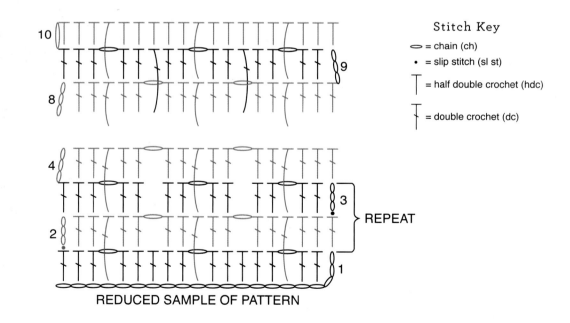

Stitch Key

⬭ = chain (ch)

• = slip stitch (sl st)

T = half double crochet (hdc)

┼ = double crochet (dc)

REDUCED SAMPLE OF PATTERN

2

fun in the
KITCHEN

Have you ever noticed how everyone seems to end up in the kitchen? From Thanksgiving dinner to Sunday morning breakfasts, the kitchen is the heart of the home. Keeping things clean is important, but there's still room for some crochet softness with cheerful dishcloths and trivets and soft, cushy rugs. If your kitchen is already set, try the rug in the bathroom or beside the bed; the dishcloths would make lovely washcloths, too!

DELIGHTFUL
dishcloth trio

Finished Size

Each dishcloth measures 9"
(23 cm) square.

Yarn

Worsted weight (#4 Medium).

Shown here: Lily Sugar'n Cream
(100% cotton; 120 yd [110 m]/
2½ oz [70 g]): stonewash (MC),
robin's egg (CC1), and tangerine
(CC2), 1 ball each.

Hook

Size H/8 (5 mm).

*Adjust hook size if necessary to
obtain the correct gauge.*

Notions

Yarn needle.

Gauge

15 sts and 9 rows = 4" (10 cm)
in dc.

Notes

+ *Carry the colors along the
  sides to minimize the number
  of ends to weave in.*

+ *The ch 3 at the beginning of a
  row counts as dc.*

Washing dishes isn't the most popular chore, but there's something about handmade dishcloths that makes it just a little more fun. Readily available cotton yarn makes them easy care and budget friendly, and a plethora of colors means you can always have ones that fit your style! All three cloths can be made with just one skein of each color.

Pattern #1

With MC, ch 33.

ROW 1: Dc in 4th ch from hook (3 skipped ch count as first dc), dc in next ch, *ch 1, sk next ch, dc in each of next 5 ch; rep from * across, ending with dc in each of last 3 ch; turn—31 sts. Drop MC to be picked up later, join CC1.

ROW 2: With CC1, ch 3 (counts as dc here and throughout), dc in each of next 2 sts, *working over ch-1 sp, dc in next skipped st 2 rows below, dc in each of next 2 sts, ch 1, sk next st, dc in each of next 2 sts; rep from * across until 1 st remains, dc in the top of ch-3; turn. Drop CC1 to be picked up later, join CC2.

ROW 3: With CC2, ch 3, dc in each of next 2 sts, *ch 1, sk next st, dc in each of next 2 sts, working over ch-1 sp, dc in next skipped st 2 rows below, dc in each of next 2 sts; rep from * across until 1 st remains, dc in the top of ch-3 tch; turn.

ROWS 4–18: Rep Rows 2–3 (7 times), then rep Row 2 once working in the following color sequence: *1 row each of MC, CC1, and CC2; rep from * throughout. Fasten off CC1 and CC2.

ROW 19: With MC, ch 1, hdc in each of first 6 sts, *working over ch-1 sp, hdc in skipped st 2 rows below, hdc in each of next 5 sts; rep from * across, ending with hdc in each of last 6 sts; turn.

Finishing

EDGING

Continuing with MC, ch 1, sc evenly around cloth, working 3 sc in each corner, join with a sl st in first sc.

Pattern #2

With A, ch 33.

ROW 1: Dc in 4th ch from hook (3 skipped chs count as first dc), dc in each ch across; turn—31 sts. Drop MC to be picked up later, join CC1.

ROW 2: With CC1, ch 3 (counts as dc here and throughout), dc in each of next 2 sts, *FPdc (see Glossary) in next st, dc in each of next 3 sts; rep from * across; turn—31 sts.

ROW 3: Ch 3, dc in each st across; turn. Drop CC1 to be picked up later, join CC2.

ROW 4: With CC2, ch 3, *FPdc in next st, dc in each of next 3 sts; rep from * across until 2 sts remain, FPdc in next st, dc in last st; turn. Drop CC2 to be picked up later, join MC.

ROW 5: With CC2, rep Row 3.

ROWS 6–17: Rep Rows 2–5 (3 times), working in the following color sequence: *2 rows each of CC1, CC2, and MC; rep from * 2 times. Fasten off CC1 and CC2.

ROW 18: With MC, rep Row 2. Do not fasten off MC.

Finishing

EDGING

Continuing with MC, ch 1, sc evenly around cloth, working 3 sc in each corner, join with a sl st in first sc.

TIP
....

Not a fan of dishcloths? Make these in soft, all-natural cotton for lovely washcloths to gift at your next baby shower or as part of a special spa gift basket.

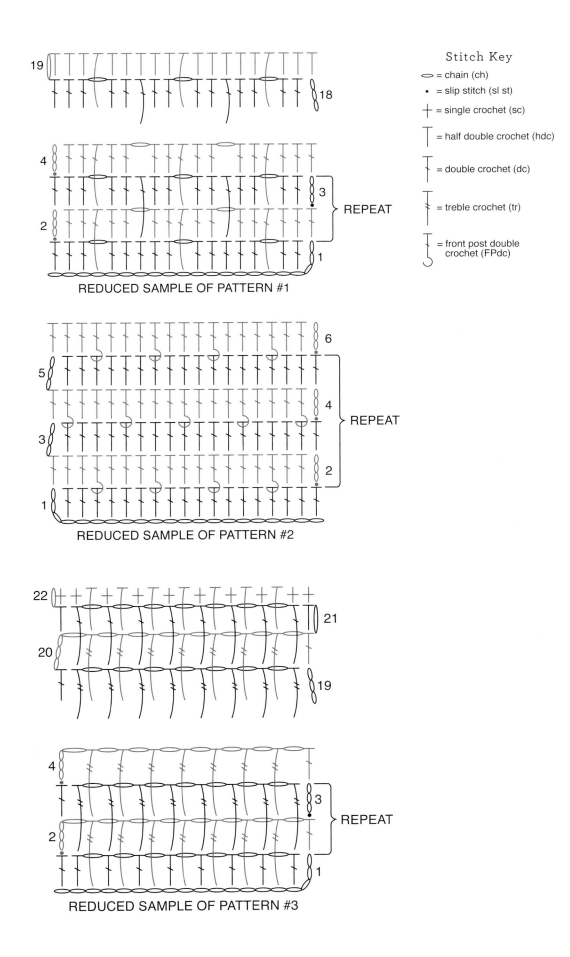

Stitch Key

⬭ = chain (ch)

• = slip stitch (sl st)

+ = single crochet (sc)

T = half double crochet (hdc)

† = double crochet (dc)

‡ = treble crochet (tr)

= front post double crochet (FPdc)

REDUCED SAMPLE OF PATTERN #1

REPEAT

REDUCED SAMPLE OF PATTERN #2

REPEAT

REDUCED SAMPLE OF PATTERN #3

REPEAT

Delightful Dishcloth Trio

Pattern #3

With MC, ch 33.

ROW 1: Dc in 4th ch from hook (3 skipped chs count as first dc), *ch 1, sk next ch, dc in next st; rep from * across; turn—31 dc. Drop MC to be picked up later, join CC1.

ROW 2: With CC1, ch 3 (counts as dc here and throughout), *ch 1, sk next st, working over ch-1 sp, tr in next skipped ch 2 rows below; rep from * across until 2 sts remain, ch 1, sk next st, dc in top of ch-3 tch; turn. Drop CC1 to be picked up later, join CC2.

ROW 3: With CC2, ch 3, *working over ch-1 sp, tr in next skipped st 2 rows below**, ch 1, sk next st; rep from * across until 2 sts remain, ending last rep at **, dc in 3rd ch of ch-4 tch; turn.

ROWS 4-20: Rep Rows 2–3 (8 times), then rep Row 2, working in the following color sequence: *1 row each of MC, CC1, and CC2; rep from * throughout. Fasten off CC1.

ROW 21: With CC2, ch 1, hdc in first st, *working over ch-1 sp, dc in next skipped st 2 rows below**, ch 1, sk next st; rep from * across until 2 sts remain, ending last rep at **, hdc 3rd ch of ch-4 tch. Fasten off CC2.

ROW 22: With MC, ch 1, sc in each of first 2 sts, *working over ch-1 sp, hdc in next skipped st 2 rows below, sc in next st; rep from * across until 1 st remains, sc in last st.

Finishing

EDGING

Continuing with MC, ch 1, sc evenly all around cloth, working 3 sc in each corner, join with a sl st in first sc. Weave in ends.

AROUND
THE TABLE
trivet

Finished Size

12½" (31.5 cm) in diameter.

Yarn

Worsted weight (#4 Medium).

Shown here: Red Heart Creme de la Creme Multis (100% cotton; 98 yd [90 m]/2 oz [57 g]): #945 orangetones (MC), 2 balls.

Worsted weight (#4 Medium).

Shown here: Red Heart Creme de la Creme Solids (100% cotton; 125 yd [114 m]/2½ oz [70 g]): #400 gray (CC1), 2 balls.

Hook

Size I/9 (5.5 mm).

Adjust hook size if necessary to obtain the correct gauge.

Notions

Stitch markers; yarn needle.

Gauge

Rnds 1–7 = 3½" (9 cm) in diameter.

Notes

+ *The yarn is held doubled throughout the pattern.*

+ *Odd-numbered rnds are unjoined to make the rnds look seamless. Even-numbered rnds are joined at the end of the rnd to hold the rnds together.*

Concentric circles will draw in your guests, mesmerized by your latest culinary creation. Or this pretty trivet will protect your tabletop and counters, and look good while doing it. Either way, it's a win-win!

Trivet

With MC, make an adjustable ring (see Glossary).

RND 1: (RS) Work 7 sc in the ring; do not join—7 sc.

RND 2: Ch 1, 2 sc in each st around, join with a sl st in first sc—14 sts.

RND 3: Working into Rnd 1 (enclosing sts of Rnd 2), 2 sc in each st around, do not join—14 sc. Fasten off MC.

RND 4: With RS facing, join CC with a sc in any st of Rnd 3, 2 sc in the next st, *sc in the next st, 2 sc in the next st; rep from * around, join with a sl st in first sc—21 sts.

RND 5: Working over Rnd 4 into sts of Rnd 3, *2 sc in the next st, sc in the next st; rep from * around—21 sts.

RND 6: Working into Rnd 5, *sc in the next 2 sts, 2 sc in the next st; rep from * around, join with a sl st in first sc—28 sts.

RND 7: Working over Rnd 6 into sts of Rnd 5, *2 sc in the next st, sc in the next 2 sts; rep from * around; break CC—28 sts.

RND 8: With RS facing, join MC with a sc in any st of Rnd 7, sc in the next 2 sts, 2 sc in the next st, *sc in the next 3 sts, 2 sc in the next st; rep from * around, join with a sl st in first sc—35 sts.

RND 9: Working over Rnd 8 into sts of Rnd 7, *2 sc in the next st, sc in the next 3 sts; rep from * around—35 sts.

RND 10: Working into Rnd 9, *sc in the next 4 sts, 2 sc in the next st; rep from * around, join with a sl st in first sc—42 sts.

RND 11: Working over Rnd 10 into sts of Rnd 9, *2 sc in the next st, sc in the next 4 sts; rep from * around—42 sts.

RND 12: Working into Rnd 11, *sc in the next 5 sts, 2 sc in the next st; rep from * around, join with a sl st in first sc—49 sts.

RND 13: Working over Rnd 12 into sts of Rnd 11, *2 sc in the next st, sc in the next 5 sts; rep from * around—49 sts. Fasten off MC.

RND 14: With RS facing, join CC with a sc in any st of Rnd 13, sc in the next 5 sts, 2 sc in the next st, *sc in the next 6 sts, 2 sc in the next st; rep from * around, join with a sl st in first sc—56 sts.

RND 15: Working over Rnd 14 into sts of Rnd 13, *2 sc in the next st, sc in the next 6 sts; rep from * around—56 sts.

RND 16: Working into Rnd 15, *sc in the next 7 sts, 2 sc in the next st; rep from * around, join with a sl st in first sc—63 sts.

RND 17: Working over Rnd 16 into sts of Rnd 15, *2 sc in the next st, sc in the next 7 sts; rep from * around—63 sts.

RND 18: Working into Rnd 17, *sc in the next 8 sts, 2 sc in the next st; rep from * around, join with a sl st in first sc—70 sts.

RND 19: Working over Rnd 18 into sts of Rnd 17, *2 sc in the next st, sc in the next 8 sts; rep from * around—70 sts.

RND 20: Working into Rnd 19, *sc in the next 9 sts, 2 sc in the next st; rep from * around, join with a sl st in first sc—77 sts.

RND 21: Working over Rnd 20 into sts of Rnd 19, *2 sc in the next st, sc in the next 9 sts; rep from * around—77 sts. Fasten off CC.

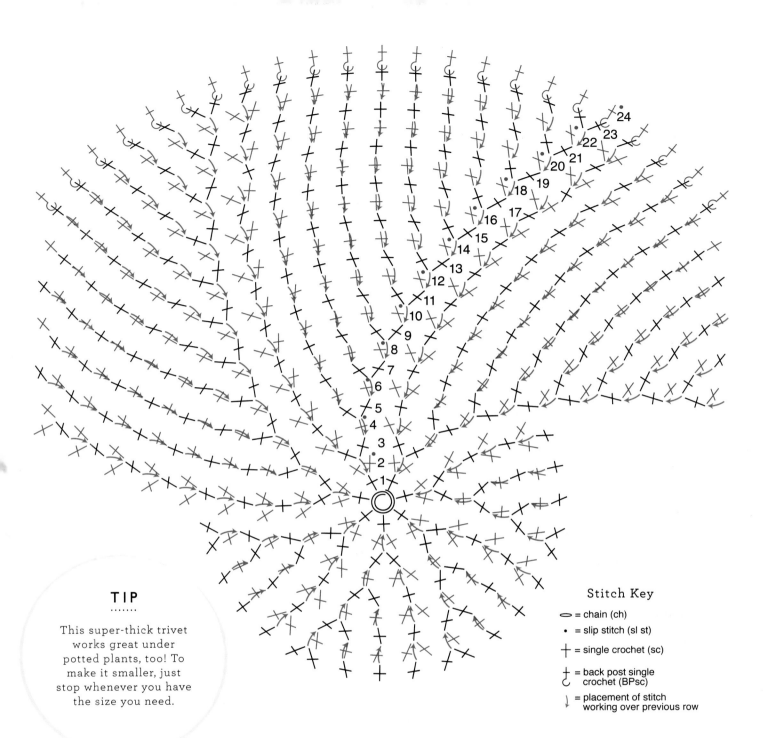

Stitch Key

⬯ = chain (ch)

• = slip stitch (sl st)

+ = single crochet (sc)

⊥ = back post single crochet (BPsc)

↓ = placement of stitch working over previous row

RND 22: With RS facing, join MC with a sc in any st of Rnd 21, sc in each of next 9 sts, 2 sc in the next st, *sc in the next 10 sts, 2 sc in the next st; rep from * around, join with a sl st in first sc—84 sts.

RND 23: Working over Rnd 22 into sts of Rnd 21, *2 sc in the next st, sc in the next 10 sts; rep from * around—84 sts. Fasten off MC.

RND 24: With RS facing, join CC with a BPsc (see Glossary) in any st of Rnd 23, BPsc in each st around, join with a sl st in first st. Fasten off CC.

Finishing

Weave in ends.

CHEF'S BEST
rug

Finished Size

27" (68.5 cm) wide × 38" (96.5 cm) long.

Yarn

Aran weight (#4 Medium).

Shown here: Red Heart with Love (100% acrylic; 370 yd [338 m]/7 oz [198 g]): #1001 white (MC), 2 skeins; #1401 pewter (CC1), #1601 lettuce (CC2), #1502 iced aqua (CC3), and #1252 mango (CC4), 1 skein each.

Hook

Size P/Q (15 mm).

Adjust hook size if necessary to obtain the correct gauge.

Notions

Yarn needle.

Gauge

5 sts and 6 rows = 4" (10 cm) in pattern.

Note

+ *Yarn is held doubled throughout; one of the yarns will always be MC.*

+ *The ch 3 at the beginning of a row counts as dc.*

Standing and cutting, standing and stirring, standing and mixing . . . cooking can be hard on your feet! This cushy rug is soft and puffy and as nice to stand on as it is to look at. Easy-care yarn means you can throw it in the wash after the little ones "help," too!

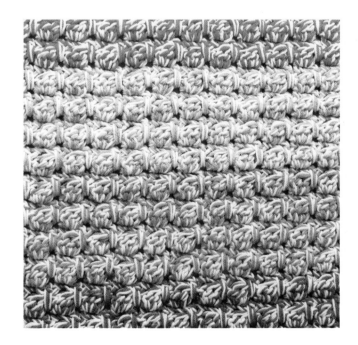

special stitches

dc3tog cluster

Yo and insert hook in indicated st, yo and draw up a loop, yo and draw through 2 loops on hook (2 loops remain on hook), yo and insert in same st, yo and draw up a loop, yo and draw through 2 loops on hook (3 loops remain on hook), yo and insert in same st, yo and draw up a loop, yo and pull through 2 loops on hook (4 loops remain on hook), yo and draw through all 4 loops on hook.

Rug

With one strand each of MC and CC1 held together as one, ch 50.

ROW 1: Sc in 2nd ch from hook, sc in each ch across; turn—49 sc.

ROW 2: Ch 3 (counts as dc here and throughout), dc3tog cluster (see Special Stitches) in next st, *ch 1, sk the next st, dc3tog cluster in next st; rep from * across until 1 st remains, dc in last st; turn—49 sts.

ROW 3: Ch 1, sc in each of first 2 sts, *working over ch-1 sp, dc in next skipped st 2 rows below, sc in next st; rep from * across until 1 st remains, sc in top of ch-3 tch; turn—49 sts.

ROWS 4–9: Rep Rows 2–3 (3 times). Fasten off CC1, join one strand CC2.

ROWS 10–17: With one strand each of MC and CC2 held together as one, rep Rows 2–3 (4 times). Fasten off CC2. Join one strand CC3.

ROWS 18–25: With one strand each of MC and CC3 held together as one, rep Rows 2–3 (4 times). Fasten off CC3. Join one strand CC4.

ROWS 26–33: With one strand each of MC and CC4 held together as one, rep Rows 2–3 (4 times). Do not fasten off.

Finishing

EDGING

Using one strand each of MC and whatever color matches the section you are crocheting into, sc evenly around outside edge of rug, join with a sl st in first sc. Weave in ends.

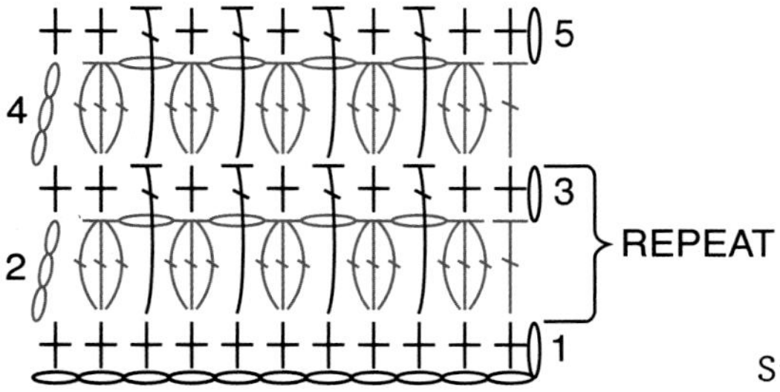

5
4
3
2
1
REPEAT

REDUCED SAMPLE OF PATTERN

Stitch Key

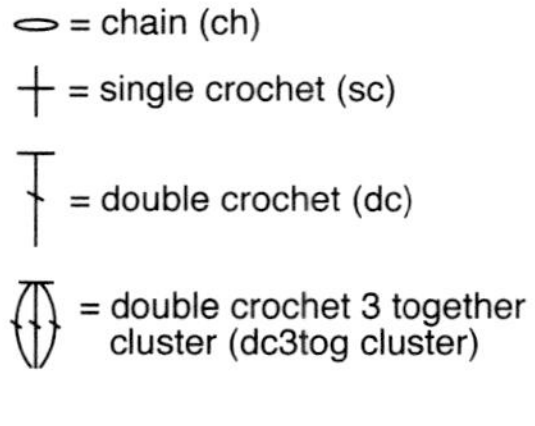

= chain (ch)
= single crochet (sc)
= double crochet (dc)
= double crochet 3 together cluster (dc3tog cluster)

TIP

Don't slip! Pick up a nonslip rug pad at your local shop and cut it to size for your handmade rugs. You can even sew them on for easy use anywhere in the home.

3
delicious
DINING ROOM

The dining room is where we all gather for the most special occasions, and there's a place for crochet here, too. Whether your dining space is a dedicated room with a giant table or a corner in the kitchen, break out your hook and add a special touch with these modern patterns.

MODERN TILE

placemats

Finished Size

Each placemat measures 17"
(43 cm) square.

Yarn

Sportweight (#2 Fine).

Shown here: Patons Grace (100%
cotton; 136 yd [124 m]/1³⁄₄ oz [50
g]): #62134 blue bayou, #62008
natural, #62027 ginger, #62048
citadel, 3 skeins each will make 4
placemats as pictured.

Hook

Size G/6 (4 mm).

*Adjust hook size if necessary to
obtain the correct gauge.*

Notions

Yarn needle.

Gauge

Rnds 1–5 = 4" (10 cm) across.

Notes

+ *Each placemat uses 2 skeins
  of a main color (MC) and 1
  skein of a contrast color (CC).
  Mix them up to match your
  own décor and preferences!*

+ *The ch 3 at the beginning of a
  row counts as dc.*

The tile look is fresh and new again, and is
being seen on fabric everywhere you look. A
graphic motif inspired these placemats, and
while it might not make the food any tastier, it
will make it look extra special!

Placemat

With MC, make an adjustable ring (see Glossary).

RND 1: (RS) Ch 3 (counts as dc here and throughout), 2 dc in ring, ch 2, [3 dc, ch 2] 3 times in ring; join with a sl st in top of ch-3 tch—12 dc; 4 ch-2 sps.

RND 2: Ch 3, dc in each of next 2 sts, (2 dc, ch 2, 2 dc) in next ch-2 sp, *dc in each of next 3 sts, (2 dc, ch 2, 2 dc) in next ch-2 sp; rep from * around, join with sl st in top of ch-3 tch—7 dc on each side.

RND 3: Ch 3, dc in the next 4 sts, (2 dc, ch 2, 2 dc) in next ch-2 sp, *dc in each of next 7 sts, (2 dc, ch 2, 2 dc) in next ch-2 sp; rep from * around, dc in each of last 2 sts, join with sl st in top of ch-3 tch—11 dc on each side.

RND 4: Ch 3, dc in the next 6 sts, (2 dc, ch 2, 2 dc) in next ch-2 sp, *dc in each of next 11 sts, (2 dc, ch 2, 2 dc) in next ch-2 sp; rep from * around, dc in each of last 4 sts, join with sl st in top of ch-3 tch—15 dc on each side.

RND 5: Ch 3, dc in each st across to next corner, (2 dc, ch 2, 2 dc) in next ch-2 sp, *dc in each st across to next corner, (2 dc, ch 2, 2 dc) in next ch-2 sp; rep from * 2 times, dc in each st across to the beginning, join with sl st in top of ch-3 tch—19 dc on each side.

RNDS 6-15: Rep Rnd 5—59 dc on each side in Rnd 15. Fasten off.

TIP

·······

These pretty place mats don't have to wait for dinner; put one under a vase of flowers to protect your table or nightstand!

Continue in pattern through Rnd 15 (59 dc on each side).

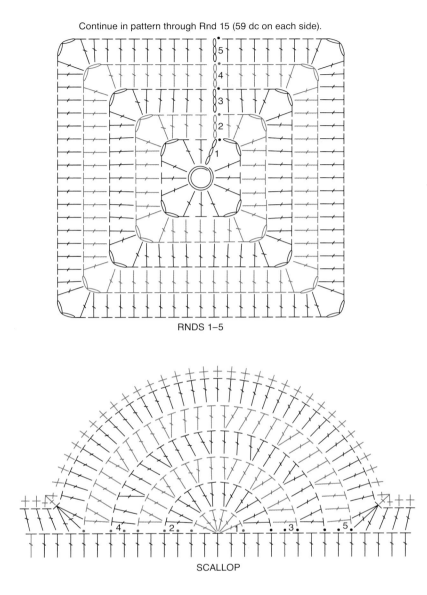

RNDS 1–5

Stitch Key

⬭ = chain (ch)

• = slip stitch (sl st)

+ = single crochet (sc)

┬ = double crochet (dc)

⋏ = single crochet 3 together (sc3tog)

⋏ = double crochet 3 together (dc3tog)

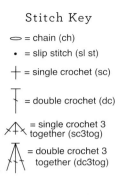

SCALLOP

EDGING

SCALLOP

Rep the following instructions on each side of the square:

ROW 1: With RS facing, join MC with a sl st in the 28th st to the left of one corner ch-2 sp, sk the next st, 6 dc in next st (this is the 30th st, or the center st of the side), sk next st, sl st in each of next 3 sts; turn—6 dc.

ROW 2 (INC ROW): Sk next 3 sl sts, 2 dc in each dc across, sk next st of the square, sl st in each of next 3 sts of the square; turn—12 dc.

ROW 3 (INC ROW): Sk next 3 sl sts, *dc in each of next st, 2 dc in next st; rep from * across, sk next st of the square, sl st in each of next 3 sts of the square; turn—18 dc.

ROW 4 (INC ROW): Sk next 3 sl sts, *dc in each of next 2 sts, 2 dc in next st; rep from * across, sk next st of the square, sl st in each of next 3 sts of the square; turn—24 dc.

ROW 5 (INC ROW): Sk next 3 sl sts, *dc in each of next 3 sts, 2 dc in next st; rep from * across, sk next st of the square, sl st in the next 3 sts of the square—30 dc sts. Fasten off MC.

Finishing

EDGING

RND 1: With RS facing, join CC in any ch-2 corner space, ch 3, (dc, ch 2, 2 dc) in next ch-2 sp, *dc in each of next 18 sts, dc3tog (see Glossary) over the next st, the st where the half circle joins the square, and the first st of the half circle, dc in each of next 3 sts, 2 dc in next st, [dc in each of next 4 sts, 2 dc in next st] 4 times, dc in each of next 4 sts, dc3tog over the next st, the st where the half circle joins the square, and the next st of the square, dc in each of next 18 sts**, (2 dc, ch 2, 2 dc) in next ch-2 sp; rep from * around, ending last rep at **, join with a sl st in top of ch-3 tch—300 dc, 4 ch-2 sps.

RND 2: Ch 1, sc in each of next 2 sts, *(sc, ch 2, sc) in the ch-2 sp, sc in the next 19 sts, sc3tog (see Glossary) over next 3 sts, sc in each of next 31 sts, sc3tog over next 3 sts**, sc in each of next 19 sts; rep from * around, ending last rep at **, sc in each of last 17 sc, join with a sl st in first sc—292 sc, 4 ch-2 sps. Fasten off CC.

Weave in ends.

TIP

....

The yardage listed is for four placemats; be sure to purchase enough yarn in the same dye lots to make as many as you need.

FAST & FESTIVE
napkin rings

Finished Size

4" (10 cm) circumference

Yarn

Sportweight (#2 Fine).

Shown here: Patons Grace (100% cotton; 136 yd [124 m]/1¾ oz [50 g]): #62134 blue bayou, #62008 natural, #62027 ginger, #62048 citadel, 1 skein each.

Hook

Size G/6 (4 mm).

Adjust hook size if necessary to obtain the correct gauge.

Notions

Yarn needle.

Gauge

5 sts = 1" (2.5 cm).

Notes

+ *Each napkin ring uses just a couple yards of a main color (MC) and contrast color (CC). You can match the placemats, or find new color combinations!*

+ *The ch 1 at the beg of a row does not count toward final st count.*

Whether they're holding cloth or paper, napkin rings let you know that your host has put forth a little extra effort—and doesn't that always feel good? These napkin rings let you play the host with the most, and your guests will never know how fun and easy they were to make! All you need is the leftover bits of yarn from the Modern Tile Placemats (page 50) to make the set!

Beg star st (beginning star stitch)

Insert hook into 2nd ch from hook and draw up a loop, insert hook into next ch and draw up a loop, skip the first st of the previous rnd, insert hook in next st and draw up a loop, yo and draw through all 4 loops on hook, ch 1.

Star st (star stitch)

Insert hook into the ch-1 that finished the previous Star Stitch and draw up a loop, insert hook in same st as last loop of previous Star Stitch and draw up a loop, skip the next st, insert hook in next st and draw up a loop, yo and draw through all 4 loops on hook, ch 1.

Napkin Ring

Starting at the bottom edge, with MC and leaving a 6" (15 cm) tail, ch 20, and without twisting ch, join into a ring with a sl st in first ch.

RND 1: Ch 1, sc in each ch around, join with a sl st in first sc—20 sc.

RNDS 2-3: Ch 1, sc in each st around, join with a sl st in first sc. Fasten off MC.

RND 4: With RS facing, join CC with a sl st in any st, ch 3, work a Beg star st (see Special Stitches), work star st (see Special Stitches) around, join with a sl st in top of beg ch-3—10 star sts.

RND 5: Ch 3, work a Beg star st, work star st around; join with a sl st in top of beg ch-3—10 star sts. Fasten off CC.

Finishing

Weave in ends.

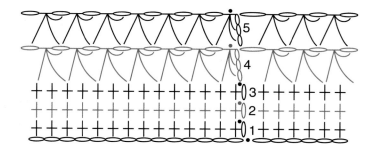

Stitch Key

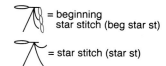

⌢ = chain (ch)

• = slip stitch (sl st)

+ = single crochet (sc)

= beginning star stitch (beg star st)

= star stitch (star st)

Finished Size

Each seat cover measures 16" (40.5 cm) square.

Yarn

Sportweight (#2 Fine).

Shown here: Patons Grace (100% cotton; 136 yd [124 m]/1¾ oz [50 g]): #62134 blue bayou, #62008 natural, #62027 ginger, #62048 citadel, 6 skeins each will make 4 seat covers as pictured.

Hook

Size J/10 (6 mm).

Adjust hook size if necessary to obtain the correct gauge.

Notions

Yarn needle.

Gauge

Each square before joining measures 7½" (19 cm) square.

Notes

+ *Each seat cover uses 4 skeins of a main color (MC) and 2 skeins of a contrast color (CC). Once again, you can mix and match as your heart desires!*

+ *Yarn is held doubled throughout.*

+ *The ch 2 at the beginning of a row does not count as a stitch.*

+ *The odd-numbered rows are the right side (RS).*

GRAPHIC TILE
seat covers

Perk up tired chairs or just add a pop of bold graphic color to your dining room with this set of seat covers. Need a little padding with your new look? Make two of each cover, sandwich a 16" (40.5 cm) square piece of foam between them, and seam around the edges.

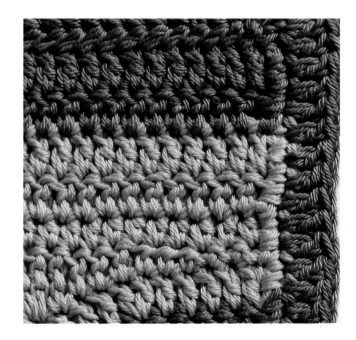

Tile *(make 4 for each seat cover)*

With MC, ch 2.

ROW 1: (RS) 3 dc in 2nd ch from hook; turn—3 dc.

ROW 2: Ch 2 (does not count as a st here and throughout), 2 dc in each dc across; turn—6 dc.

ROW 3: Ch 2, dc in first st, 2 dc in next st, *dc in next st, 2 dc in next st; rep from * around; turn—9 dc.

ROW 4: Ch 2, dc in first 2 sts, 2 dc in next st, *dc in next 2 sts, 2 dc in next st; rep from * across; turn—12 dc.

ROW 5: Ch 2, dc in each of first 3 sts, 2 dc in the next st, *dc in each of next 3 sts, 2 dc in the next st; rep from * across; turn—15 dc.

ROW 6: Ch 2, dc in each of first 4 sts, 2 dc in next st, *dc in each of next 4 sts, 2 dc in next st; rep from * across; turn—18 sts. Fasten off MC, join CC.

ROW 7: With CC, ch 2, dc in each of first 5 sts, 2 dc in next st, *dc in each of next 5 sts, 2 dc in next st; rep from * across—21 dc.

ROW 8: Ch 1, sc in each of first 3 sts, hdc in each of next 3 sts, dc in each of next 3 sts, tr in next st, 5 tr in next st, tr in next st, dc in each of next 3 sts, hdc in each of next 3 sts, sc in each of last 3 sts; turn—25 sts.

ROW 9: Ch 1, hdc in each of first 12 sts, 5 dc in next st, hdc in each of last 12 sts; turn—29 sts.

ROW 10: Ch 2, dc in each of first 14 sts, 5 dc in next st, dc in each of last 14 sts; turn—33 dc.

ROW 11: Ch 2, dc in each of first 16 sts, 5 dc in next st, dc in each of last 16 sts; turn—37 dc. Fasten off CC, join MC.

ROW 12: With MC, ch 2, dc in each of first 18 sts, 5 dc in next st, dc in each of last 18 sts; turn—41 dc.

ROW 13: Ch 2, dc in each of first 20 sts, (2 dc, tr, 2 dc) in next st, dc in each of last 20 sts—45 sts. Fasten off CC.

Finishing

Lay out tiles in a square RS up, with center st of last row of each tile meeting in the center. With MC, whipstitch (see Glossary) tiles together.

EDGING

Rnd 1 of edging is worked using MC in MC sts and CC in CC sts of square.

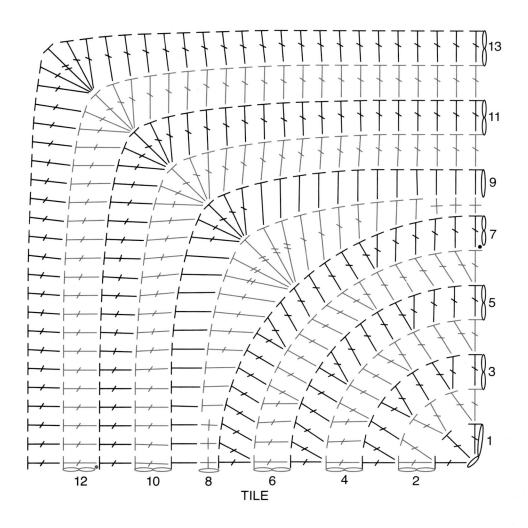

RND 1: With RS facing, join CC in first CC row on one side of square, ch 1, *sc evenly across side of CC rows, finishing last st with MC, sc evenly across side of MC rows, finishing last st with CC; rep from * around, working (sc, ch 2, sc) in each corner; with MC, join with a sl st in first sc. Fasten off CC.

RND 2: With MC, ch 2, dc in each st around, working 3 dc in each corner ch-2 sp, join with a sl st in first sc. Fasten off MC. Weave in ends.

TIES

Place seat covers on chairs to decide placement. Use MC yarn to add chain ties to your seat covers long enough to secure them to your chair backs.

Stitch Key

⬯ = chain (ch)

• = slip stitch (sl st)

╋ = single crochet (sc)

⊤ = half double crochet (hdc)

⊤ = double crochet (dc)

⸸ = treble crochet (tr)

4
BATHROOM
retreat

The bathroom is certainly utilitarian, but it's also a private retreat, a place where you can go to be alone (or at least try when there are toddlers around). Adding special touches with crochet can turn your everyday bathroom into a lovely and relaxing space to start and end your day!

SPA
jar covers

Finished Size

9" (23 cm) circumference x 4" (10 cm) tall

Yarn

DK weight (#3 Light).

Shown here: Cascade Ultra Pima (100% cotton; 220 yd [201 m]/ 3½ oz [100 g]): #3724 armada (MC), #3729 gray (CC1), #3762 spring green (CC2), #3718 natural (CC3), 1 hank each.

Hook

Size F/5 (3.75 mm).

Adjust hook size if necessary to obtain the correct gauge.

Notions

Tapestry needle; 3 pint canning jars.

Gauge

3" (7.5 cm) diameter after Rnd 5.

Notes

+ *The ch 1 or ch 2 at the beg of a rnd does not count as a stitch.*

These handy containers aren't just for the bathroom; make a set for your craft space to sort your crochet hooks and show them off, too! Each jar cover uses only a few yards of each color, so mix and match as your heart desires. Even after making a set of three, there is plenty of yarn left over to make the Luxury Towel Touches (page 70) as well!

special stitches

2-dc cluster

Yo and insert hook in indicated stitch, pull up a loop, yo and pull through first 2 loops on hook (2 loops remain on hook), yo and insert hook in same st, pull up a loop, yo and pull through first 2 loops on hook (3 loops remain on hook), yo and pull through all 3 loops.

V-st (V-stitch)

(Dc, ch 4, dc) in next st.

Jar Cover

With MC, make an adjustable ring (see Glossary).

RND 1: Ch 1 (does not count as a st here and throughout), 10 hdc in ring; join with a sl st in first hdc—10 hdc.

RND 2: Ch 1, 2 hdc in each hdc around; join with a sl st in first hdc—20 hdc.

RND 3: Ch 1, hdc in first st, 2 hdc in next st, *hdc in next st, 2 hdc in next st; rep from * around, join with a sl st in first hdc—30 hdc.

RND 4: Ch 1, hdc in each of first 2 sts, 2 hdc in next st, *hdc in each of next 2 sts, 2 hdc in next st; rep from * around, join with a sl st in first hdc—40 hdc.

RND 5: Ch 1, hdc in each of first 3 sts, 2 hdc in next st, *hdc in each of next 3 sts, 2 hdc in next st; rep from * around, join with a sl st in first hdc—50 hdc.

RND 6: Ch 2 (does not count as a st here and throughout), dc in first st, *ch 2, sk next 4 sts, V-st (see Special Stitches) in next st, ch 2, sk next 4 sts**, dc in next st; rep from * around, ending last rep at **, join with a sl st in first dc—5 V-sts.

RND 7: Ch 1, sk first st, *2 sc in next ch-2 sp, 5 sc in next ch-4 sp, 2 sc in next ch-2 sp; rep from * around, join with a sl st in first sc—45 sc.

RND 8: Ch 2, dc in first st, sk next st, *2-dc cluster (see Special Stitches) in each of next 5 sts, sk next 2 sts**, dc in next st; rep from * around, ending last rep at **, join with a sl st in first dc—30 sts.

RND 9: Ch 1, sc between first 2 sts, *ch 1, sc between next 2 sts; rep from * around, ch 1, join with a sl st in first sc—30 sc, 30 ch. Fasten off MC.

RND 10: With RS facing, join CC1 with a sl st in last ch-1 sp of previous rnd, ch 2, dc in same ch-1 sp, *ch 2, sk next 3 sc, V-st in next ch-1 sp, ch 2, sk next 3 sc**, dc in next ch-1 sp; rep from * around, ending last rep at **, join with a sl st in first dc—5 V-sts.

RNDS 11–21: Rep Rnds 7–10 (2 times), joining CC2 and CC3 where applicable on each rep; then rep Rnds 7–9 (1 time). Fasten off.

Finishing

Weave in ends.

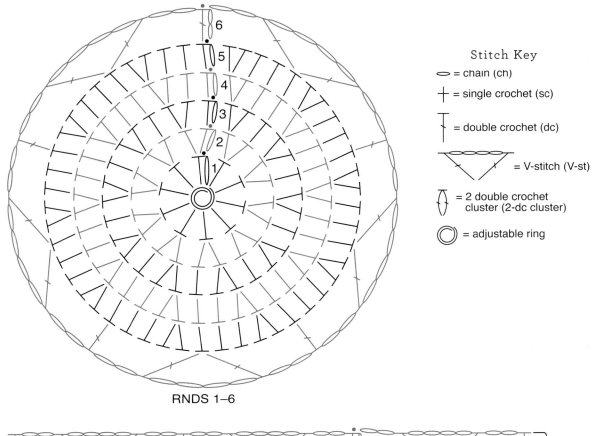

RNDS 1–6

Stitch Key

◯ = chain (ch)

╂ = single crochet (sc)

┬ = double crochet (dc)

= V-stitch (V-st)

= 2 double crochet cluster (2-dc cluster)

◎ = adjustable ring

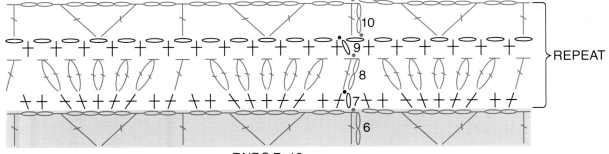

RNDS 7–10

REPEAT

LUXURY TOWEL
touches

Finished Size

1" (2.5 cm) wide × 15½" (39.5 cm) long.

Yarn

DK weight (#3 Light).

Shown here: Cascade Ultra Pima (100% cotton; 220 yd [201 m]/3½ oz [100 g]): #3724 armada or #3762 spring green (MC) and natural (CC), 1 hank each will make 3 towel trims as pictured.

Hook

Size F/5 (3.75 mm).

Adjust hook size if necessary to obtain the correct gauge.

Notions

Stitch marker; yarn needle; sewing needle and thread; 4 hand towels.

Gauge

18 sts = 4" (10 cm) in pattern.

Whether you're looking to impress your guests or liven up everyday linens, these pretty edgings are just the thing to make plain hand towels stand out above the rest. This pattern is written to fit a standard 16-inch (40.5 cm) wide hand towel, but you can start with any odd number of chains to customize it to fit bath towels, bath sheets, and even pillowcases! Use the leftover bits of yarn from the Spa Jar Covers (page 66) for a coordinated look.

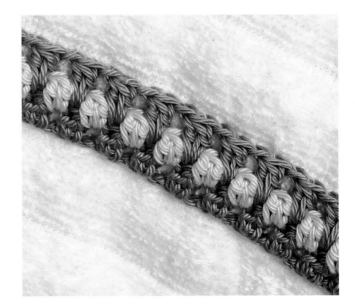

special stitches

2-dc cluster

Yo and insert hook in indicated stitch, draw up a loop, yo and draw through first 2 loops on hook (2 loops remain on hook), yo and insert hook in same st, draw up a loop, yo and draw through first 2 loops on hook (3 loops remain on hook), yo and draw through all 3 loops on hook.

Trim

With MC, ch 73.

ROW 1: (WS) *2-dc cluster (see Special Stitches) in 3rd ch from hook, ch 1, sk 1 ch; rep from * across until 1 ch remains, 2-dc cluster in last ch; turn—36 clusters. Drop loop from hook and place on a st marker.

ROW 2: With RS facing, join CC with a sl st in first ch-1 sp, ch 2, 2-dc cluster in same ch-1 sp, *ch 1, sk next st, 2-dc cluster in next ch-1 sp; rep from * across, do not turn—35 clusters.

ROW 3: Pick up dropped loop of MC, remove st marker, with MC, ch 2, 2-dc cluster in first cluster of Row 1, *ch 1, sk next st of Row 2, working over ch-1 sp in Row 2, 2-dc cluster in next st in Row 1; rep from * across, ending with ch 1, 2-dc cluster in last st of Row 1—36 2-dc clusters. Fasten off.

Finishing

Weave in ends. Use sewing needle and thread to sew to hand towel.

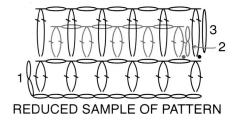

REDUCED SAMPLE OF PATTERN

Stitch Key

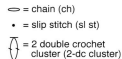

= chain (ch)

• = slip stitch (sl st)

= 2 double crochet cluster (2-dc cluster)

Finished Size

20" (51 cm) wide × 30" (76 cm) long.

Yarn

Aran weight (#4 Medium).

Shown here: Willow Yarns Cub (60% cotton, 40% acrylic; 88 yd [80 m]/1¾ oz [50 g]): #1 eggshells (MC), 6 skeins; #3 mist (CC1), 4 skeins; #10 lily pad (CC2), 2 skeins.

Hook

Size L/11 (8 mm).

Adjust hook size if necessary to obtain the correct gauge.

Notions

Yarn needle.

Gauge

1 square = 5" (12.5 cm) square.

Notes

+ *Yarn is held doubled throughout.*

+ *The ch 1 at the beg of a row does not count toward final st count*

STEP ON IN
rug

Two strands of yarn held together means the motifs on this stylish rug work up quickly—and make the rug super luxurious, too. Ultra cushy, ultra plush, and ultra modern!

special stitches

hdc/sc2tog

Yo, insert hook in next st, draw up a loop, insert hook in next st, draw up a loop, yo and draw through all loops on hook—1-st dec made.

sc/hdc2tog

Insert hook in next st, draw up a loop, yo, insert hook in next st, draw up a loop, yo and draw through all loops on hook—1-st dec made.

hdc/sc/hdc3tog

Yo, insert hook in next st, draw up a loop, insert hook in next st, draw up a loop, yo, insert hook in next st, draw up a loop, yo and draw through all loops on hook—2-st dec made.

Square (make 16 using CC1 as CC; make 8 using CC2 as CC)

With MC, ch 2.

ROW 1: (RS) Sc in 2nd ch from hook; turn—1 sc.

ROW 2: Ch 1 (does not count as a st here and throughout), (hdc, sc, hdc) in sc; turn—3 sts.

ROW 3: Ch 1, (hdc, sc) in first st, sc in next st, (sc, hdc) in last st; turn—5 sts.

ROW 4: Ch 1, (hdc, sc) in first st, sc in each st across to last st, (sc, hdc) in last st; turn—7 sts.

ROWS 5-9: Rep Row 4—17 sts. Fasten off MC.

ROW 10: With WS facing, join CC with a sl st in first st, ch 1, hdc/sc2tog (see Special Stitches) over first 2 sts, sc in each of next 13 sts, sc/hdc2tog (see Special Stitches) over last 2 sts; turn—15 sts.

ROW 11: Ch 1, hdc/sc2tog over first 2 sts, sc in each st across to last 2 sts, sc/hdc2tog over last 2 sts; turn—13 sts.

ROWS 12-16: Rep Row 11—3 sts at end of last row.

ROW 17: Ch 1, hdc/sc/hdc3tog (see Special Stitches) over next 3 sts—1 st. Fasten off CC.

Finishing

Arrange squares following Assembly Diagram or in desired pattern. Sew together squares using mattress stitch (see Glossary). Weave in ends.

TIP

Play with the layout of the squares before you sew them together to create your own look. And be sure to add your nonslip rug pad for safety!

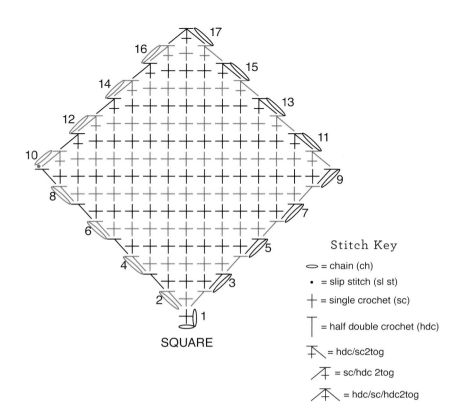

SQUARE

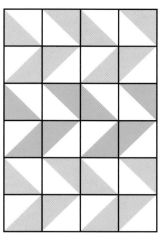

ASSEMBLY DIAGRAM

Stitch Key

◯ = chain (ch)

• = slip stitch (sl st)

+ = single crochet (sc)

T = half double crochet (hdc)

⊤ = hdc/sc2tog

⊤ = sc/hdc 2tog

⊼ = hdc/sc/hdc2tog

5

cozy up in the
BEDROOM

At the end of a long day, the bedroom is a welcome retreat from the world. A place to get cozy, comfy, and, well, whatever else you like to do in the bedroom! These crochet patterns will make your bedroom a place where you'll be happy to let your hair down, from busy weekday nights to lazy weekend mornings.

Finished Size

64" (162.5 cm) wide × 68" (173 cm) long.

Yarn

Chunky weight (#5 Bulky).

Shown here: Willow Burrow Bulky (75% cotton, 25% wool; 131 yd [120 m]/3½ oz [100 g]): #2 frosting (MC), #16 delicious (CC1), #29 vamp (CC2), #35 deep purple (CC3), 5 balls each.

Hook

Size M-N/13 (9 mm).

Adjust hook size if necessary to obtain the correct gauge.

Notions

Yarn needle.

Gauge

8 sts and 5 rows = 4" (10 cm) in dc.

Notes

+ *When crocheting along the side of a set of 5 rows, work as follows: 2 dc in the side of the first row, dc in the side of the second row, 2 dc in the side of the third row, 1 dc in the side of the fourth row, and 2 dc in the side of the fifth row—8 sts worked evenly along the side of 5 rows.*

+ *The ch 2 at the beginning of each row does not count as a stitch, and is not crocheted into.*

LOG CABIN RETREAT
throw

The Log Cabin pattern is a classic, in both crochet and quilting. Comforting and homey, yet graphic and modern, it can reflect your personality with the simplest changes. Mix up the order of color changes to get new looks. This pattern is also a great stash-buster!

Throw

FIRST SECTION

With MC, ch 10.

ROW 1: (RS) Dc in 3rd ch from hook, dc in each remaining ch across; turn—8 dc.

ROWS 2-5: Ch 2 (does not count as a st here and throughout), dc in each dc across; turn—8 dc. Rotate 90 degrees rather than flipping the fabric.

SECOND SECTION

ROW 1: Working along the sides of Rows 5 through 1, ch 2, work 8 dc evenly spaced across (see note on p. 81); turn—8 dc.

ROWS 2-5: Ch 2, dc in each dc across; turn—8 dc. At end of Row 5, fasten off MC and rotate 90 degrees.

THIRD SECTION

ROW 1 (INC ROW): With RS facing, join CC1 with a sl st in in last st of Second Section, ch 2, working along the sides of Rows 5 through 1 of Second Section, work 8 dc evenly spaced across, work 8 dc across the foundation ch of First Section; turn—16 dc.

ROWS 2-5: Ch 2, dc in each dc across; turn—16 sts. At the end of Row 5, rotate 90 degrees.

FOURTH SECTION

ROW 1: Ch 2, work 16 dc evenly spaced across sides of 10 rows of Third and First Sections; turn—16 dc.

ROWS 2-5: Ch 2, dc in each dc across; turn—16 dc. At end of Row 5, fasten off CC1 and rotate 90 degrees.

FIFTH SECTION

ROW 1 (INC ROW): With RS facing, join CC2 with a sl st in last st of last section, ch 2, work 24 dc evenly spaced across previous 5 rows, across top of next 8 sts, and across side of last 5 rows; turn—24 dc.

ROWS 2-5: Ch 2, dc in each dc across; turn—24 dc. At end of Row 5, rotate 90 degrees.

SIXTH SECTION

ROW 1: Ch 2, work 24 dc evenly spaced across previous 5 rows, across top of next 8 sts, and across side of last 5 rows; turn—24 dc.

ROWS 2-5: Ch 2, dc in each dc across; turn—24 dc. At end of Row 5, fasten off CC2 and rotate 90 degrees.

SEVENTH SECTION

ROW 1 (INC ROW): With RS facing, join CC3 with a sl st in last st of last section, ch 2, work 32 dc evenly spaced across previous 5 rows, across tops of sts, and across side of last 5 rows; turn—32 dc.

ROWS 2-5: Ch 2, dc in each st across; turn—32 dc. At the end of Row 5, rotate 90 degrees.

EIGHTH SECTION

ROW 1: Ch 2, work 32 dc evenly spaced across previous 5 rows, across tops of 8 sts, and across side of last 5 rows; turn—32 dc.

ROWS 2-5: Ch 2, dc in each st across; turn—32 dc. At the end of Row 5, fasten off CC3 and rotate 90 degrees.

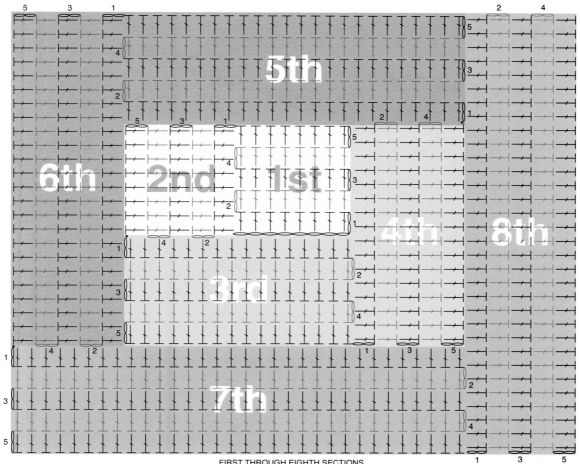

FIRST THROUGH EIGHTH SECTIONS

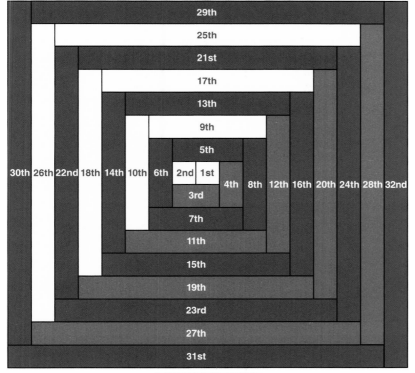

CONSTRUCTION DIAGRAM

Stitch Key

⬭ = chain (ch)

• = slip stitch (sl st)

⊤ = double crochet (dc)

NINTH–32ND SECTIONS

Rep Seventh and Eighth Sections, working in the following color sequence: *2 sections each of MC, CC1, CC2, and CC3; rep from * 3 times, increasing by 8 sts every 2 sections, ending with 128 sts in last 2 sections. Fasten off CC3.

Finishing

EDGING

With RS facing, join MC in any corner st, sc evenly around blanket, working 3 sc in each corner, join with a sl st in first sc. Fasten off. Weave in ends.

BREAKFAST IN BED
pillow

Finished Size

16" (40.5 cm) square.

Yarn

Chunky weight (#5 Bulky).

Shown here: Willow Burrow Bulky (75% cotton, 25% wool; 131 yd [120 m]/3½ oz [100 g]): #2 frosting, 5 balls.

Hook

Size J/10 (6 mm).

Adjust hook size if necessary to obtain the correct gauge.

Notions

18" (45.5 cm) square pillow form; yarn needle.

Gauge

12 sts and 10 rows = 4" (10 cm) in popcorn pattern.

Notes

+ *The fabric should measure approximately 32" (81.5 cm) long and 15" (38 cm) wide before assembly.*

+ *The ch 2 at the beginning of a row does not count as a st and is not crocheted into.*

This overstuffed pillow features amazing monochromatic texture. The popcorn shell stitches remind me of tiny croissants—a luxury breakfast in bed every day! And when you're ready for a change, just flip it over for a whole different look.

special stitches

Psh (Popcorn shell)

Work 9 dc in indicated st, then drop active loop of last dc, insert hook in top of first dc, replace active loop on hook, push popcorn downward so backs of sts show, then draw loop through top of first st, ch 1.

Pillow

Ch 46.

ROW 1: Sc in 2nd ch from hook, sc in each ch across; turn—45 sc.

ROW 2: Ch 2 (does not count as a st here and throughout), dc in first st, *psh (see Special Stitches) in next st, dc in each of next 5 sts; rep from * across until 2 sts remain, pop in next st, dc in last st; turn—8 pshs.

ROW 3: Ch 1, sc in each st across; turn—45 sc.

ROW 4: Ch 2, dc in each of first 4 sts, *psh in next st, dc in next 5 sts; rep from * until 5 sts remain, psh in next st, dc in each of last 4 sts; turn—7 pshs.

ROW 5: Ch 1, sc in each st across; turn—45 sc.

ROW 6: Ch 2, dc in first st, *psh in next st, dc in next 5 sts; rep from * across until 2 sts remain, psh in next st, dc in last st; turn—8 pshs.

ROW 7: Ch 1, sc in each st across; turn—45 sts.

ROW 8: Ch 2, dc in first 4 sts, *psh in next st, dc in each of next 5 sts; rep from * across until 5 sts remain, psh in next st, dc in each of last 4 sts; turn—7 pshs.

ROWS 9–39: Rep Rows 5–8 (7 times), then rep Rows 5–7 (1 time).

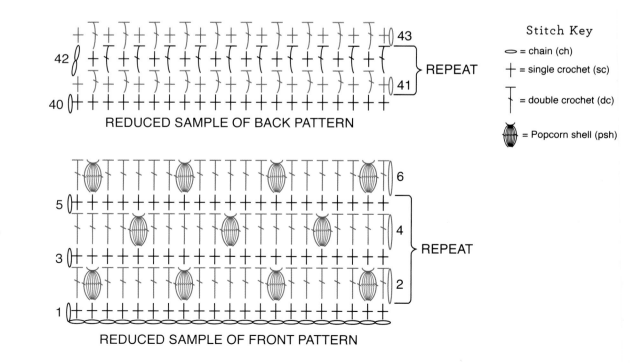

REDUCED SAMPLE OF BACK PATTERN

Stitch Key

⌒ = chain (ch)

+ = single crochet (sc)

T = double crochet (dc)

⬮ = Popcorn shell (psh)

REDUCED SAMPLE OF FRONT PATTERN

QUICK CROCHET *for the Home*

ROW 40: Ch 1, sc in first st, dc in next st, *sc in next st, dc in next st; rep from * across until 1 st remains, sc in the last st; turn—45 sts.

ROW 41: Ch 2, dc in the first st, sc in next st, *dc in next st, sc in next st; rep from * across until 1 st remains, dc in last st; turn—45 sts.

ROWS 42–79: Rep Rows 40–41 (19 times). Fasten off, leaving a long tail.

Finishing

Fold fabric in half at Row 39, so that the pop sts are facing out, and Row 79 is lined up with the foundation chain at the bottom of Row 1. Using long tail, whipstitch (see Glossary) Row 79 to foundation chain, then continue and seam up the side. Insert pillow form in open side, and use additional yarn to whipstitch final side closed. Weave in ends.

BLING
ring bowls

Bedside tables and dresser tops can become a dumping ground of earrings, bobby pins, loose change . . . all types of odds and ends! A simple set of nesting bowls gets all blinged out with sparkly thread and keeps all those bits organized and looking neat. Each hank of yarn makes lots of bowls!

Finished Size

Smallest bowl is 3" (7.5 cm) in diameter.

Yarn

Aran weight (#4 Medium).

Shown here: Willow Yarns Field (53% cotton, 47% linen; 176 yd [161 m]/3½ oz [100 g]): #6 cattails (MC1), #14 iris (MC2), #3 sand (MC3), 1 hank each.

Lace weight (#1 Super Fine).

Shown here: Kreinik Twist (65% polyester, 35% rayon; 273 yd [250 m]): #002 gold (CC), 1 cone.

Hook

Size E/4 (3.5 mm).

Adjust hook size if necessary to obtain the correct gauge.

Notions

Stitch marker; yarn needle.

Gauge

First 6 rnds = 2" (5 cm) in diameter.

Note

+ *This pattern is worked in a spiral, without joins at the end of each rnd, except for one rnd of each bowl, where there is a join and a turn. Use a stitch marker to mark the first st of each rnd.*

Small Bowl

With MC, make an adjustable ring (see Glossary).

RND 1: (WS) Work 6 sc in ring, do not join—6 sc. Work in a spiral, marking beginning of rnd and moving marker up as work progresses.

RND 2: 2 sc in each st around—12 sc.

RND 3: *Sc in next st, 2 sc in next st; rep from * around—18 sc.

RND 4: *2 sc in next st, sc in each of next 2 sts; rep from * around—24 sc.

RND 5: *Sc in each of next 3 sts, 2 sc in next st; rep from * around—30 sc.

RND 6: *Sc in each of next 4 sts, 2 sc in next st; rep from * around—36 sc.

RND 7: *2 sc in next st, sc in each of next 11 sts; rep from * around—39 sc.

RND 8: Sc in the first 12 sts, 2 sc in the next st, *sc in next 12 sts, 2 sc in next st; rep from * around—42 sc.

RND 9: Sc in each of next 7 sts, 2 sc in next st, [sc in next 13 sts, 2 sc in next st] 2 times, sc in each of last 6 sts—45 sc.

RND 10: *Sc in each of next 14 sts, 2 sc in next st; rep from * around, join with sl st in next sc; turn—48 sc.

RND 11: With RS facing, join CC, with 1 strand each of MC and CC held together as one, ch 1, sc in each st around—48 sc.

Note: Continue to work in a spiral as before, marking beg of each rnd.

RNDS 12–14: Sc in each st around. At end of last rnd, join with a sl st in next st. Fasten off. Weave in ends.

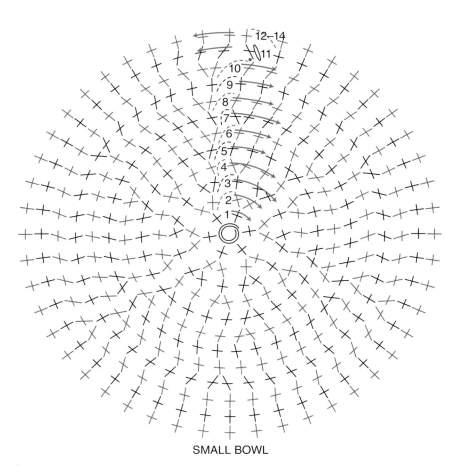

SMALL BOWL

Stitch Key

⬯ = chain (ch)

+ = single crochet (sc)

◎ = adjustable ring

⟵ = direction of work

TIP

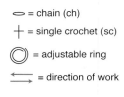

You can also put these in the kitchen, bathroom, or anywhere you need a place for things to land. And don't forget the craft room; they're perfect for keeping your pretty stitch markers close at hand!

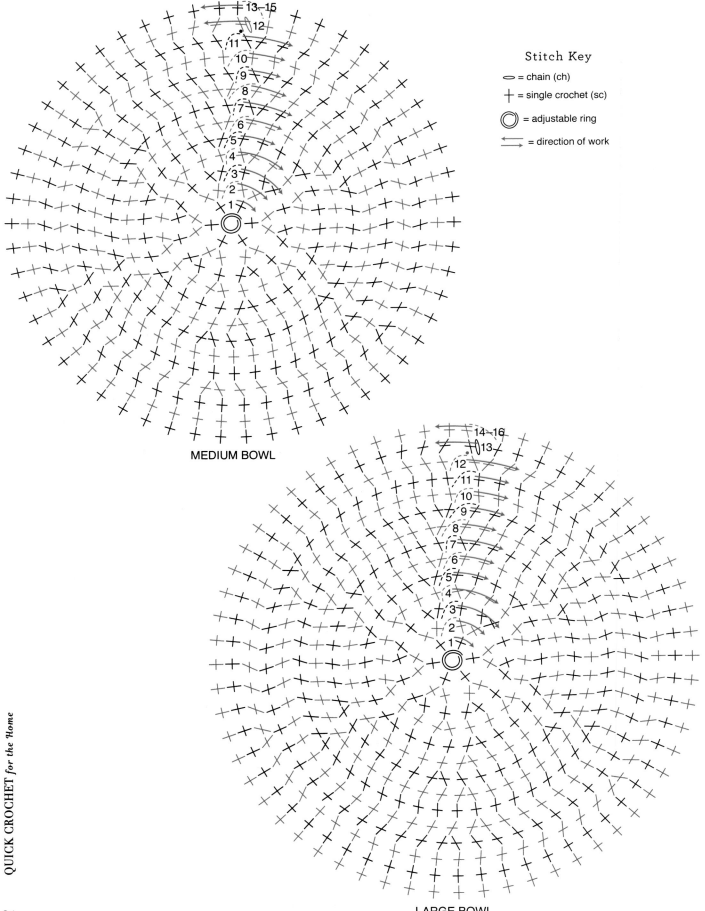

Stitch Key

⬭ = chain (ch)

✛ = single crochet (sc)

◎ = adjustable ring

⟵ = direction of work

13–15

12

11

10

9

8

7

6

5

4

3

2

1

MEDIUM BOWL

14–16

13

12

11

10

9

8

7

6

5

4

3

2

1

LARGE BOWL

Medium Bowl

RNDS 1-6: With MC, rep Rnds 1-6 of small bowl.

RND 7: *2 sc in next st, sc in next 5 sts; rep from * around—42 sc.

RND 8: *Sc in each of next 13 sts, 2 sc in the next st; rep from * around—45 sc.

RND 9: *2 sc in next st, sc in each of next 14 sts; rep from * around—48 sc.

RND 10: Sc in each of first 8 sts, 2 sc in the next st, *sc in each of next 15 sts, 2 sc in the next st; rep from * until 7 sts remain, sc in each of last 7 sts—51 sc.

RND 11: *2 sc in the next st, sc in each of next 16 sts; rep from * around, join with sl st in next sc; turn—54 sc.

RND 12: With RS facing, join CC, with 1 strand each of MC and CC held together as one, ch 1, sc in each st around—54 sc.

Note: Continue to work in a spiral as before, marking beg of each rnd.

RNDS 13-15: Sc in each st around. At end of last rnd, join with a sl st in next st. Fasten off. Weave in ends.

Large Bowl

RNDS 1-7: With MC, rep Rnds 1-7 of medium bowl.

RND 8: *Sc in each of next 6 sts, 2 sc in next st; rep from * around—48 sc.

RND 9: *Sc in the each of next 15 sts, 2 sc in the next st; rep from * around—51 sc.

RND 10: *2 sc in next st, sc in each of next 16 sts; rep from * around—54 sc.

RND 11: Sc in each of first 8 sts, 2 sc in the next st, *sc in each of next 17 sts, 2 sc in the next st, rep from * until 9 sts remain, sc in each of last 9 sts—57 sc.

RND 12: *2 sc in the next st, sc in each of next 18 sts; rep from * around, join with sl st in next sc; turn—60 sc.

RND 13: With RS facing, join CC, with 1 strand each of MC and CC held together as one, ch 1, sc in each st around—60 sc.
Note: Continue to work in a spiral as before, marking beg of each rnd.

RNDS 14-16: Sc in each st around. At end of last rnd, join with a sl st in next st. Fasten off.

Finishing

Weave in ends.

6
KIDS
these days

Crocheting for little ones is one of the most traditional things you can do with your hook—but that doesn't mean your projects have to look old-fashioned! Trendy, modern looks are right at home in the nursery or child's bedroom and will grow right along with them. They work great in other rooms of the house, too.

Finished Size

38" (96.5 cm) wide × 40" (101.5 cm) long.

Yarn

Worsted weight (#4 Medium).

Shown here: Plymouth Encore Worsted (75% acrylic, 25% wool; 200 yd [183 m]/3½ oz [100 g]): #218 champagne (MC), #896 petal yellow (CC1), #472 cantaloupe (CC2), #461 living coral (CC3), #212 cinnabar (CC4), 2 balls each.

Hook

Size J/10 (6 mm).

Adjust hook size if necessary to obtain the correct gauge.

Gauge

13 sts and 8 rows = 4" (10 cm) in dc.

Notes

+ *The ch 2 at the beginning of each row does not count as a stitch, and is not crocheted into.*

+ *Do not break the yarn unless directed; you will have up to six balls of yarn in use at once.*

+ *Change colors by pulling the loop of the new color through the last two loops of the previous color to finish the last st of the previous color, and drop the previous color to pick up when you return to that spot in the next row.*

+ *When starting a new color several stitches after you finished with it in the previous row, crochet over it until it's time to pick it up again.*

+ *When starting a new color several stitches before you finished with it in the previous row, pull it to the new location to finish the last st of the previous color, and crochet over it with the next several stitches.*

CHEVRON CUDDLES *blanket*

Inspired by classic chevron quilts, where the fabric is sewn in strips and then lined up to create the ripple pattern, this cozy blanket is worked side to side to achieve a similar effect—without the sewing. This also eliminates the increases or decreases that can make traditional crochet chevron patterns so tricky. Here, it's all double crochet stitches!

special stitches

Twisted dc

Yo, insert hook in next st, yo, draw yarn through 2 loops on hook (2 loops remain on hook), turn the hook 360 degrees (counterclockwise for right-handed crocheters, clockwise for left-handed crocheters), then yo and draw through last 2 loops to finish st.

Blanket

With MC, ch 122.

ROW 1: Dc in 3rd ch from hook, dc in each of next 19 ch finishing last st with CC1, dc in each of next 25 ch finishing last st with CC2, dc in each of next 25 ch finishing last st with CC3, dc in each of next 25 sts finishing last st with CC4, dc in each of last 25 sts; turn—120 dc. Row 1 of Chart complete.

ROWS 2-27: Work even in dc following Chart for color changes.

ROWS 28-75: Rep Rows 4-27 (2 times). Fasten off all colors except 2nd ball of MC.

Finishing

Note: To work evenly along sides, work a rep of 2 sc in each of next 2 rows, then work 1 sc in the side of the next row.

RND 1: With MC, ch 1, sc in each st across, ch 2, work 125 sc evenly spaced across side of blanket, ch 2, working across foundation ch, sc in each ch across, ch 2, work 125 sc evenly spaced across side of blanket, ch 2, join with a sl st in first sc—490 sc, 4 ch-2 corners.

RND 2: Ch 2, twisted dc (see Special Stitches) in each st around, working (2 twisted dc, ch 2, 2 twisted dc) in each corner ch-2 sp; join with a sl st in first st. Fasten off MC.

Weave in ends.

COLOR KEY

☐ = MC
☐ = CC1
☐ = CC2
▧ = CC3
■ = CC4

REPEAT

27 25 23 21 19 17 15 13 11 9 7 5 3 1

CHART

26 24 22 20 18 16 14 12 10 8 6 4 2

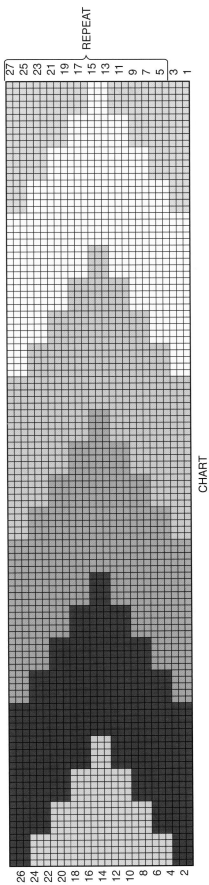

Chevron Cuddles Blanket

Crayola

ROBOT

I Love You to the MOON and BACK   tiger tales

THE THREE BILLY GOATS GRUFF

Finished Size

7½" (19 cm) tall × 9" (23 cm) diameter.

Yarn

Shown here: Plymouth Encore Worsted (75% acrylic, 25% wool; 200 yd [183 m]/3½ oz [100 g]): #463 purl gray (MC), 2 balls; #459 lagoon (CC1), 2 balls; #154 blue haze (CC2), 1 ball.

Hook

Size K/10½ (6.5 mm).

Adjust hook size if necessary to obtain the correct gauge.

Gauge

First 5 rnds = 4" (10 cm) in diameter.

Notes

+ *Yarn is held doubled throughout pattern.*

+ *The ch 2 at the beginning of a rnd does not count as a st.*

+ *Do not turn until instructed in the pattern (turns only used in Rnds 10–18).*

+ *For the first ldc (see Glossary) of each rnd, insert hook into 2nd ch of ch-3 to pull up first loop, then work as usual.*

TOT'S BEST
toy basket

One thing I've learned as a parent is that kids come with a lot of stuff! From the top of the changing table to the big kid's shelf, baskets are a mom or dad's best friend. Go for looks that will grow with your child and add more as their collection of trinkets and stuffed animals and action figures grows!

special stitches

Ldc (Linked Double Crochet)

Insert hook in front horizontal bar of previous dc or ldc st and pull up a loop, insert hook in next st and pull up a loop, (yo and pull through 2 lps) twice.

BPsc (back post single crochet)

Insert hook from back to front to back again around the post of next st, yo and draw yarn though, yo, draw yarn through 2 loops on hook.

Basket

With MC, make an adjustable ring (see Glossary).

RND 1 (WS): Work 9 hdc in ring; join with a sl st in first hdc—9 hdc.

RND 2: Ch 2 (does not count as a st here and throughout), 2 hdc in each st around; join—18 hdc.

RND 3: Ch 2, hdc in first st, *2 hdc in next st, hdc in next st**; rep from * around, ending last rep at **, join with a sl st in first hdc—27 hdc.

RND 4: Ch 2, hdc in each of first 2 sts, *2 hdc in next st**, hdc in each of next 2 sts, 2 hdc in next st; rep from * around, ending last rep at **, join with a sl st in first hdc—36 sts.

RND 5: Ch 2, 2 hdc in first st, *hdc in each of next 3 sts**, 2 hdc in next st; rep from * around, ending last rep at **, join with a sl st in first hdc—45 sts.

RND 6: Ch 2, hdc in each of first 4 sts, *2 hdc in next st**, hdc in each of next 4 sts; rep from * around, ending last rep at **, join with a sl st in first hdc—54 sts.

RND 7: Ch 2, hdc in each of first 5 sts, *2 hdc in next st**, hdc in each of next 5 sts; rep from * around, ending last rep at **, join with a sl st in first hdc—63 sts.

RND 8: Ch 2, hdc in each of first 6 sts, *2 hdc in next st**, hdc in each of next 6 sts; rep from * around, ending last rep at **, join with a sl st in first hdc—72 sts.

RND 9: Ch 2, hdc in each of first 7 sts, *2 hdc in next st**, hdc in each of next 7 sts; rep from * around, ending last rep at **, join with a sl st in first hdc—81 sts.

RND 10: Ch 2, 2 hdc in first st, *hdc in each of next 8 sts**, 2 hdc in next st; rep from * around, join with a sl st in first hdc; turn—90 sts.

RND 11: (RS) Ch 2, dc in each st around; join with a sl st in first dc; turn—90 sts.

RND 12: (WS) Ch 1, sc in each st around; join with a sl st in first hdc; turn—90 sts.

RND 13: (RS) Ch 2, dc in first st, *FPtr (see Glossary) in next corresponding dc 2 rows below**, dc in next st; rep from * around, ending last rep at **, join with a sl st in first dc; turn—90 sts.

RND 14: (WS) Rep Rnd 12.

RND 15: (RS) Ch 2, FPtr in first corresponding dc 2 rows below, *dc in next st, FPtr in next corresponding dc 2 rows below; rep from * around, ending last rep at **, join with a sl st in first FPtr; turn—90 sts.

RNDS 16-19: Rep Rnds 12-15. Do not turn after Rnd 19.

RND 20: (RS) Ch 1, sc in each st around; join with a sl st in first sc, do not turn. Fasten off MC.

RND 21: With RS facing, join CC1 in blo (see Glossary) of first sc, ch 3 (counts as first ldc), ldc (see Glossary) in blo of each st around; join with a sl st in first ldc—90 ldc.

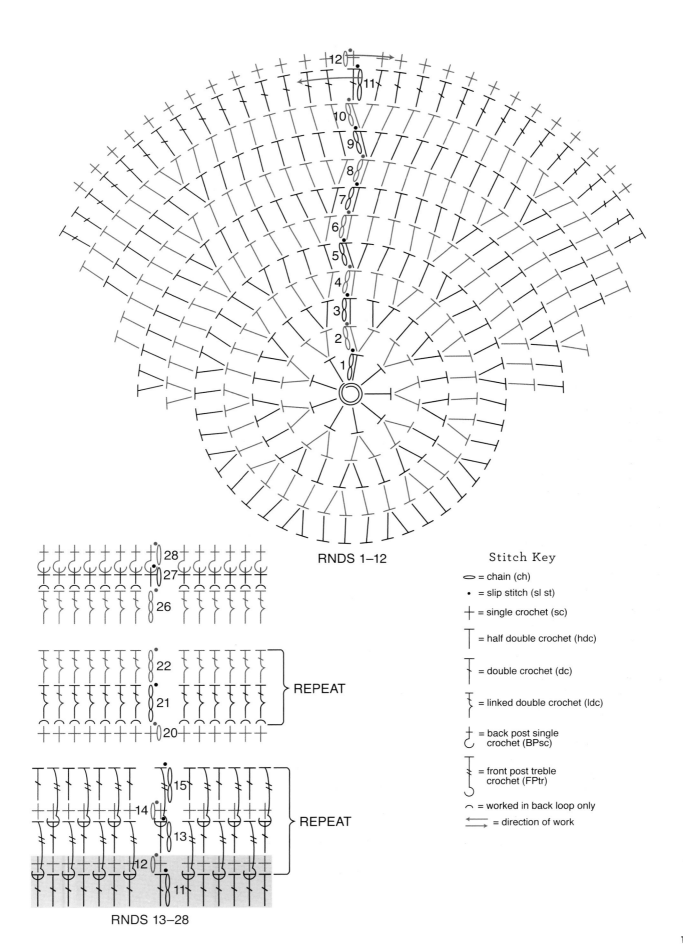

RNDS 1–12

28
27
26

22
21
20
} REPEAT

15
14
13
12
11
} REPEAT

RNDS 13–28

Stitch Key

⬯ = chain (ch)

• = slip stitch (sl st)

+ = single crochet (sc)

T = half double crochet (hdc)

† = double crochet (dc)

⨍ = linked double crochet (ldc)

+ = back post single crochet (BPsc)

= front post treble crochet (FPtr)

⌢ = worked in back loop only

⟷ = direction of work

RND 22: Ch 3, ldc in both loops of each st around; join with a sl st in first ldc. Fasten off CC1.

RNDS 23–24: With CC2, rep Rnds 21–22. Fasten off CC2.

RNDS 25–26: With CC1, rep Rnds 21–22. Fasten off CC1.

RND 27: With RS facing, join MC with a sl st in first st of previous rnd, ch 1, sc in blo of each st around; join with a sl st in first sc—90 sc.

RND 28: Ch 1, BPsc (see Glossary) in each st around; join with a sl st in first sc—90 BPsc. Fasten off MC.

Finishing

Weave in ends.

Finished Size

Fits one pair of 9" (23 cm) metal bookends.

Yarn

Aran weight (#4 Medium).

Shown here: Lion Brand Vanna's Choice (100% acrylic; 170 yd [156 m]/3 ½oz [100 g]): #151 charcoal gray (MC), 2 balls; #133 brick (CC1), 1 ball; #100 white (CC2), 1 ball.

Hook

Size H/8 (5 mm).

Adjust hook size if necessary to obtain the correct gauge.

Notions

Stitch markers; fiberfill; yarn needle; set of two 9" (23 cm) metal bookends.

Gauge

16 sts and 20 rows = 4" (10 cm) in sc.

Notes

+ *Make the parts of the bookends in the order listed and assemble them when directed in the pattern.*

SMART AS A FOX
bookends

Reading is important—for kids as well as adults—and the earlier the better! These charming bookends dress up a pair of standard 9-inch (23 cm) metal bookends, found at most big box stores and office supply shops, and turn them into something to help give your child's imagination a head start!

Covers *(make 2 of each part)*

Part 1 (will face out, with fox attached)

Starting at top edge with MC, ch 25.

ROW 1: (RS) Sc in 2nd ch from hook, sc in each ch across; turn—24 sc.

ROWS 2–45: Ch 1, sc in each st across; turn—24 sc.

ROW 46: Ch 1, sc in blo (see Glossary) of each st across; turn—24 sts.

Note: This row will make the "crease" in the cover where it transitions from vertical to horizontal.

ROWS 47–59: Ch 1, sc in each st across; turn—24 sts. Fasten off.

Part 2 (will face in, toward the books)

ROWS 1–45: Rep Rows 1–45 of Part 1. Set cover pieces aside, unassembled.

Ears *(make 2)*

BACK

Starting at bottom edge with CC1, ch 6.

ROW 1: (RS) Sc in 2nd ch from hook, sc in each ch across; turn—5 sc.

ROWS 2–3: Ch 1, sc in each st across; turn—5 sc.

ROW 4: Ch 1, sc2tog (see Glossary) over first 2 sts, sc in next st, sc2tog over last 2 sts; turn—3 sts.

ROW 5: Ch 1, sc3tog (see Glossary) over next 3 sts—1 st. Fasten off.

FRONT

Starting at bottom edge with CC2, rep Rows 1–5 of back. Fasten off.

WITH RS facing up, place front on top of back; working through double thickness, join MC with a sl st in bottom right-hand corner, ch 1, sc evenly around ear pieces to bottom left-hand corner. Set ears aside.

Nose

Starting at top of nose with MC, make an adjustable ring (see Glossary), ch 2, 3 dc in ring. Fasten off, leaving long tail. Set nose aside.

Head

Note: Head is worked in a spiral, without joining the rnds or chaining at the beginning of each rnd; use a st marker to mark first st of each rnd.

Starting at top of head with CC1, make an adjustable ring.

RND 1: Work 6 sc in ring, do not join, work in a spiral marking beg of rnd, moving marker up as work progresses—6 sc.

RND 2: 2 sc in each st around—12 sc.

RND 3: *Sc in next st, 2 sc in next st; rep from * around—18 sc.

RND 4: *Sc in each of next 2 sts, 2 sc in the next st; rep from * around—24 sc.

RND 5: *Sc in each of next 3 sts, 2 sc in the next st; rep from * around—30 sc.

RND 6: *2 sc in each of next st, sc in the next 4 sts; rep from * around—36 sc.

RND 7: *Sc in each of next 8 sts, 2 sc in the next st; rep from * around—40 sc.

RNDS 8–11: Sc in each st around. Fasten off CC1, join CC2.

RND 12: With CC2, sc in each st around—40 sc.

RND 13: Sc in each st around.

RND 14: *Sc in each of next 8 sts, sc2tog over next 2 sts; rep from * around—36 sts.

RND 15: *Sc in each of next 4 sts, sc2tog over next 2 sts; rep from * around—30 sts. Drop loop from hook and place st marker in loop to secure.

USE MC to sew on eyes as shown, then sew ears and nose to head as pictured. Remove st marker and reinsert hook in active loop at end of Rnd 15.

RND 16: *Sc2tog over next 2 sts, sc in each of next 3 sts; rep from * around—24 sts.

RND 17: *Sc in each of next 2 sts, sc2tog over next 2 sts; rep from * around—18 sts. Drop loop from hook and place st marker in loop to secure.

Stuff head with fiberfill, remove st marker and reinsert hook in active loop at end of Rnd 17.

RND 18: *Sc2tog over next 2 sts, sc in next st; rep from * around—12 sts. Fasten off, leaving a long tail. Stuff remainder of head with fiberfill and set aside.

Body

Note: Body is worked in a spiral, without joining the rnds or chaining at the beginning of a rnd; use a st marker to mark first st of each rnd.

RNDS 1–6: Starting at top of body, with CC1, rep Rnds 1–6 of head.

RNDS 7–20: Continue in a spiral, sc in each st around—36 sts. Fasten off, leaving a long tail. Set body aside.

CHEST/BELLY

Starting at top edge with CC2, ch 4.

ROW 1: Sc in 2nd ch from hook, sc in each ch across; turn—3 sc.

ROW 2 (INC ROW): Ch 1, 2 sc in first st, sc in next st, 2 sc in last st; turn—5 sc.

ROW 3 (INC ROW): Ch 1, sc in each st across; turn—5 sc.

ROW 4 (INC ROW): Ch 1, 2 sc in first st, sc in each of next 3 sts, 2 sc in last st; turn—7 sc.

ROWS 5–11: Rep Row 3—7 sc. Do not fasten off.

EDGING

With CC2, ch 1, sc evenly along side of piece, around top curve, and down the other side to the opposite end of Row 11. Fasten off, leaving a long tail. Set chest/belly aside.

Paws *(make 2)*

Starting at bottom of paw, with MC, ch 4.

ROW 1: Hdc in 2nd ch from hook, 2 dc in next ch, hdc in last ch. Fasten off, leaving a long tail.

SEW HEAD to body. Sew chest/belly to body. Sew paws to body at base of chest/belly. Stuff body with fiberfill. Sew head/body combo to horizontal section of 1 Part 1 of cover. Set aside.

Tail

Note: Tail is worked in a spiral, without joining the rnds or chaining at the beginning of a rnd; use a st marker to mark first st of each rnd.

Starting at bottom of tail, with CC1, make an adjustable ring (see Glossary).

RND 1: Work 6 sc in ring, do not join, work in a spiral as before—6 sc.

RND 2: *Sc in the next st, 2 sc in next st; rep from * around—9 sc.

RND 3: *Sc in each of next 2 sts, 2 sc in next st; rep from * around—12 sc.

RND 4: *Sc in each of next 3 sts, 2 sc in next st; rep from * around—15 sc.

RND 5: *Sc in each of next 4 sts, 2 sc in next st; rep from * around—18 sc.

RND 6: *2 sc in the next st, sc in each of next 5 sts; rep from * around—21 sc.

RND 7: *Sc in each of next 6 sts, 2 sc in next st; rep from * around—24 sc.

RND 8: *Sc in each of next 7 sts, 2 sc in next st; rep from * around—27 sc.

RND 9: *Sc in each of next 8 sts, 2 sc in next st; rep from * around—30 sc.

RND 10: *2 sc in the next st, sc in the next 9 sts; rep from * around—33 sc.

RND 11: Sc in each of first 5 sts, *2 sc in the next st, sc in the next 10 sts; rep from * 1 time, 2 sc in next st, sc in each of last 5 sts—36 sts.

RNDS 12-28: Sc in each st around—36 sts. Fasten off CC1, join CC2.

RND 29: With CC2, sc in each st around—36 sts.

RND 30: *Sc in each of next 10 sts, sc2tog (see Glossary) over next 2 sts; rep from * around—33 sts.

RND 31: *Sc2tog over next 2 sts, sc in each of next 9 sts; rep from * around—33 sts. Drop loop from hook and place st marker in loop to secure.

USE CC1 to sew beginning of tail to vertical piece of 2nd Part 1 of cover, and sew middle of tail to horizontal piece of same Part 1, adding a slight curve toward the front. Stuff tail with fiber-fill, maintaining the curve. Remove st marker and reinsert hook in active loop at end of Rnd 31.

RND 32: *Sc in each of next 8 sts, sc2tog over next 2 sts; rep from * around—27 sts.

RND 33: *Sc2tog over next 2 sts, sc in each of the next 7 sts; rep from * around—24 sts.

RND 34: Sc in each of first 3 sts, sc2tog over next 2 sts, *sc in each of next 6 sts, sc2tog over next 2 sts; rep from * 1 time, sc in each of the last 3 sts—21 sts.

RND 35: *Sc in each of next 5 sts, sc2tog over next 2 sts; rep from * around—18 sts.

RND 36: *Sc2tog over next 2 sts, sc in each of next 4 sts; rep from * around—15 sts.

RND 37: Sc in the next 3 sts, sc2tog over next 2 sts; rep from * around—12 sts.

RND 38: *Sc2tog over next 2 sts, sc in each of next 2 sts; rep from * around—9 sts.

RND 39: *Sc in next st, sc2tog over next 2 sts; rep from * around. Fasten off, leaving a long tail—6 sts. Stuff remainder of tail with fiberfill. Weave tail through last rnd of sts, gather together, and secure.

Finishing

EDGINGS

Place one Part 2 piece of cover over one Part 1 piece, aligning top edge. With Part 1 facing, join MC with a sl st in bottom right-hand corner of Part 2 piece, ch 1, sc evenly up side to corner, 3 sc in corner, sc in each st across top, 3 sc in corner, sc evenly up other side edge to bottom corner of Part 2. Fasten off, leaving bottom open to slip over metal bookends. Repeat with other cover parts. Weave in ends.

ABBREVIATIONS

beg	begin; begins; beginning		**rep**	repeat; repeating
bet	between		**rnd(s)**	round(s)
blo	back loop only		**RS**	right side
CC	contrasting color		**sc**	single crochet
ch(s)	chain(s)		**sk**	skip
cm	centimeter(s)		**sl**	slip
cont	continue(s); continuing		**sl st**	slip(ped) stitch
dc	double crochet		**sp(s)**	space(s)
dec	decrease(s); decreasing; decreased		**st(s)**	stitch(es)
dtr	double treble crochet		**tch**	turning chain
flo	front loop only		**tog**	together
foll	follows; following		**tr**	treble crochet
g	gram(s)		**WS**	wrong side
hdc	half double crochet		**yd**	yard(s)
inc	increase(s); increasing; increased		**yo**	yarn over
lp(s)	loop(s)		*****	repeat starting point
MC	main color		**()**	alternative measurements and/or instructions; work instructions within parentheses in place directed
m	marker; meter(s)			
mm	millimeter(s)		**[]**	work bracketed instructions a specified number of times
patt(s)	pattern(s)			
pm	place marker			
rem	remain(s); remaining			

GLOSSARY

Back Loop Only (blo)

The back loop is the loop at the top of the stitch that is farthest away from the crocheter.

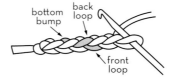

Making an Adjustable Ring

Make a large loop with the yarn **(figure 1)**. Holding the loop with your fingers, insert hook in loop and pull working yarn through loop **(figure 2)**. Yarn over hook, pull through loop on hook. Continue to work indicated number of stitches in loop **(figure 3**; shown in single crochet). Pull on yarn tail to close loop **(figure 4)**.

figure 1

figure 2

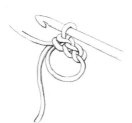

figure 3

figure 4

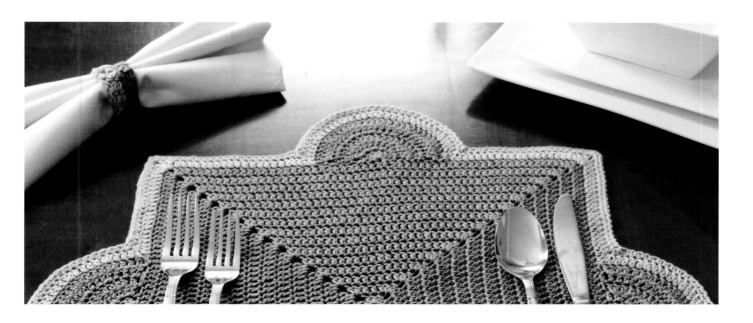

Stitches

CHAIN (CH)

Make a slipknot and place it on crochet hook. *Yarn over hook and draw through loop on hook. Repeat from * for the desired number of stitches.

SLIP STITCH (SL ST)

*Insert hook in stitch, yarn over and draw loop through stitch and loop on hook; repeat from *.

SINGLE CROCHET (SC)

Insert hook in second chain from hook, yarn over and pull up loop, yarn over and draw through both loops on hook. *Insert hook in next chain, yarn over and pull up loop, yarn over and draw through both loops on hook; repeat from *.

HALF DOUBLE CROCHET (HDC)

*Yarn over, insert hook in stitch (figure 1), yarn over and pull up loop (3 loops on hook), yarn over (figure 2) and draw through all loops on hook (figure 3); repeat from *.

figure 1   figure 2   figure 3

DOUBLE CROCHET (DC)

*Yarn over hook, insert hook in a stitch, yarn over hook and draw up a loop (3 loops on hook; **figure 1**), yarn over hook and draw it through 2 loops **(figure 2)**, yarn over hook and draw it through remaining 2 loops on hook **(figure 3)**. Repeat from *.

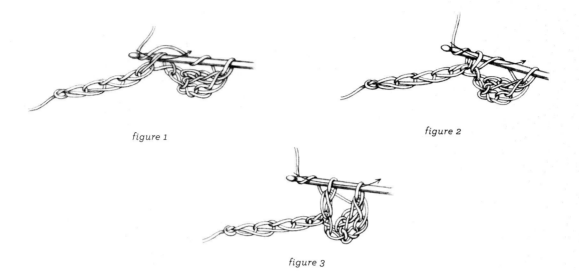

figure 1

figure 2

figure 3

TREBLE CROCHET (TR)

*[Wrap yarn around hook] 2 times, insert hook in next indicated stitch, yarn over hook and draw up a loop (4 loops on hook; **figure 1**), yarn over hook and draw it through 2 loops **(figure 2)**, yarn over hook and draw it through next 2 loops, yarn over hook and draw it through the remaining 2 loops on hook **(figure 3)**. Repeat from *.

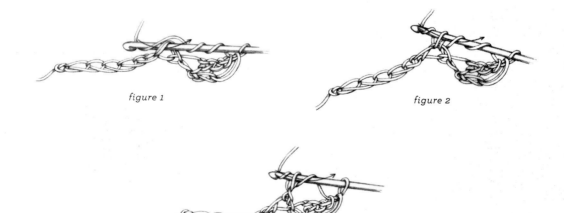

figure 1

figure 2

figure 3

BACK POST SINGLE CROCHET (BPSC)

Insert hook from back to front to back again around post of corresponding stitch below, yarn over and pull up loop, yarn over and draw through 2 loops on hook.

FRONT POST DOUBLE CROCHET (FPDC)

Yarn over hook, insert hook from front to back to front again around post of stitch indicated, yarn over hook and pull up a loop (3 loops on hook), [yarn over hook and draw through 2 loops on hook] 2 times—1 FPdc made.

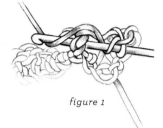

figure 1

FRONT POST TREBLE CROCHET (FPTR)

[Yarn over hook] 2 times, insert hook in specified stitch from front to back, right to left, around the post (or stem). Yarn over hook, pull through work only, *yarn over hook, pull through 2 loops on hook. Rep from * 2 times—1 FPtr made.

LINKED DOUBLE CROCHET (LDC)

Insert hook in front horizontal bar of previous dc or ldc st and pull up a loop **(figure 1)**, insert hook in next st and pull up a loop **(figure 2)**, [yo and pull through 2 loops] 2 times **(figures 3–5)**.

figure 1

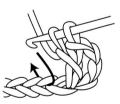

figure 2

figure 3

figure 4

figure 5

Decreases

SINGLE CROCHET TWO TOGETHER (SC2TOG)

Insert hook in stitch and draw up a loop. Insert hook in next stitch and draw up a loop. Yarn over hook **(figure 1)**. Draw through all 3 loops on hook **(figures 2 and 3)**—1 stitch decreased.

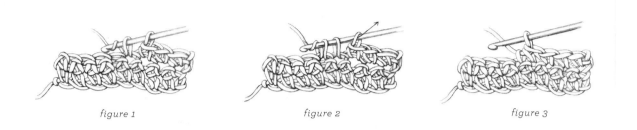

figure 1   *figure 2*   *figure 3*

SINGLE CROCHET THREE TOGETHER (SC3TOG)

[Insert hook in next stitch, yarn over, pull loop through stitch] 3 times (4 loops on hook). Yarn over and draw yarn through all 4 loops on hook. Completed sc3tog—2 stitches decreased.

DOUBLE CROCHET TWO TOGETHER (DC2TOG)

[Yarn over, insert hook in next stitch, yarn over and pull up loop **(figure 1)**, yarn over, draw through 2 loops] 2 times **(figure 2)**, yarn over, draw through all loops on hook **(figure 3)**—1 stitch decreased **(figure 4)**.

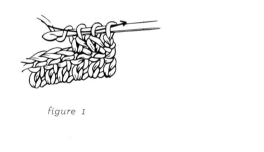

figure 1

figure 2

figure 3

figure 4

DOUBLE CROCHET THREE TOGETHER (DC3TOG)

[Yarn over, insert hook in next stitch, yarn over and pull up loop, yarn over, draw through 2 loops] 3 times (4 loops on hook), yarn over, draw through all loops on hook—2 stitches decreased.

Seaming

MATTRESS STITCH

Hold both pieces to be joined with the right sides facing and edges parallel to each other. Use threaded yarn needle to *insert the needle vertically under and out a stitch (or post) on the first piece and then under and out of the corresponding stitch (or post) of the 2nd piece. Repeat from * to end of seam.

WHIPSTITCH

With right sides (RS) of work facing and working through edge stitches, bring threaded needle out from back to front, along edge of piece.

YARN SOURCES

Berroco

1 Tupperware Drive
Suite. 4
North Smithfield, RI 02896-6815
(401) 769-1212
berroco.com

Cascade

1224 Andover Park E
Tukwila, WA 98188
(206) 574-0440
cascadeyarns.com

Lily

320 Livingstone Avenue South
P. O. Box 40
Listowel, ON
Canada N4W 3H3
(888) 368-8401
yarnspirations.com/lily

Lion Brand

135 Kero Road
Carlstadt, NJ 07072
(800) 661-7551
lionbrand.com

Patons

320 Livingstone Avenue South
P. O. Box 40
Listowel, ON
Canada N4W 3H3
(888) 368-8401
yarnspirations.com/patons

Plymouth Yarn

500 Lafayette Street
Bristol, PA 19007
(215) 788-0459
plymouthyarn.com

Red Heart

Coats & Clark Consumer Services
P.O. Box 12229
Greenville, SC 29612-0229
(800) 648-1479
redheart.com

Willow Yarns

Willow Yarns Customer Care
2800 Hoover Road
Stevens Point, WI 54492
(855) 279-4701
willowyarns.com

DEDICATION

To Geoff, Riley, Braedon, and Connor
*- for your encouragement, inspiration, love,
support, and all the laughs.*

Acknowledgments

The past few years have been an absolute whirlwind—who would've thought a simple hobby would become so... much? Crochet has allowed me to travel, make new friends, and support my family, and I am ever so grateful to everyone who has played a part in making Moogly what it is today.

Thank you to the friends, who told me what I made was good enough to share with others. Thank you to the fans, who somehow found me from day one and encouraged me to keep designing and exploring. Thank you to all the amazing crochet professionals who accepted me and welcomed me into their club—it's such an honor to be one of you, and count so many of you among my friends.

Thank you to Kerry, Michelle, Maya, and all the other people who helped bring this book into being, for all your hard work—and for being patient with me while I learned how to write one!

Thank you to my family—I am so lucky to have a spouse who believed in and encouraged me from the get-go, and kids who are always ready to tell me what to make next (and where I'm going wrong!) To my mom, who supported my craftiness from an early age, and to my dad, who passed away last year. He found the whole crochet business thing pretty confusing, but was proud nonetheless—I wish he'd gotten to see this book. To Nicholas, Cynthia, Chad, Kaitlin, and Ross, who all helped make me who I am today.

And lastly, thank you! Without you, my life would be very different, and a lot more boring.

About the author

Tamara Kelly is the designer and blogger behind Mooglyblog.com, where she shares her crochet patterns (and a few knitting ones too), video tutorials, and whatever other fun yarny goodies she can find. Her patterns have been published in *I Like Crochet* magazine and several book compilations. She is a Craftsy Instructor and award winning blogger, and lives in Iowa with her helpful husband, three occasionally helpful kids, and one very unhelpful dog.

METRIC CONVERSION CHART

To convert	to	multiply by
Inches	Centimeters	2.54
Centimeters	Inches	0.4
Feet	Centimeters	30.5
Centimeters	Feet	0.03
Yards	Meters	0.9
Meters	Yards	1.1

KEEP ON STITCHING...
for your home and beyond

Interweave Presents Classic Crochet Blankets: 18 Timeless Patterns to Keep You Warm

by Interweave Editors

Curl up under handmade warmth and crocheted comfort! In this book you'll find some of our favorite, timeless patterns for crochet afghans, blankets, and throws.

ISBN: 978-1-63250-359-6
Price: $19.99

3 Skeins or Less - Modern Baby Crochet: 18 Crochet Baby Garments, Blankets, Accessories, and More!

by Sharon Zientara

This fresh collection of patterns offers perfect crochet designs for your littlest loved ones. Even better, each pattern only requires 1, 2, or 3 skeins of yarn!

ISBN: 978-1-63250-152-3
Price: $ 22.99

Crochet to Calm: Stitch and De-Stress with 18 Colorful Crochet Patterns

by Interweave Editors

Discover the most rewarding way to de-stress at the end of a hectic day—crochet! From home accents to cozy wearables, all the projects in this book are quick to make, so you'll have plenty of time to try them all.

ISBN: 978-1-63250-495-1
Price: $21.99